Overcoming Stage Fright in Everyday Life

Overcoming Stage Fright in Everyday Life

Joyce Ashley

Three Rivers Press • New York

Complete set of permissions can be found on page 173

Published by Three Rivers Press, 201 East 50th Street, New York, New York 10022. Member of the Crown Publishing Group.

Originally published in hardcover by Clarkson Potter/Publishers, 1996. First paperback edition printed in 1997.

http://www.randomhouse.com/

Random House, Inc. New York, Toronto, London, Sydney, Auckland

THREE RIVERS PRESS and colophon are trademarks of Crown Publishers, Inc.

Manfactured in the United States of America

Library of Congress Cataloging-in-Publication Data

Ashley, Joyce.
Overcoming stage fright in everyday life / Joyce Ashley.–1st ed.
Includes bibliographical references.
1. Anxiety. 2. Speech anxiety. 3. Stage fright–Case studies.
4. Self-help techniques. 5. Jungian psychology. I. Title.
BF575.A6A76 1996
616.85′225–dc20   96–410
                                                                    CIP

ISBN 0-609-80097-3

10 9 8 7 6 5 4 3 2 1

First Paperback Edition

For Hilde Kirsch, C. A. Meier, Sylvia Perera,
and Edward C. Whitmont, who helped me redeem my fate.

And for Julie, Sarah, Annie, and Jenny,
who enrich my days.

Acknowledgments

THIS BOOK HAS BEEN five years in the making and would not have been possible without the support of many people.

I am grateful to Sylvia Perera for her generosity of spirit and inspired analytic work.

I deeply appreciate the encouragement of Estelle Weinrib and Gilda Frantz.

My thanks to Walter Odajnyk for his suggestion that I expand and publish this work; to Gertrud Ujhely for her careful criticism of an early draft; to John Beebe and Beverly Zabriskie for their belief in the merits of the final product.

Thanks also to Daniel Yankelovich and his late wife, Mary, who designed the research; to Hazel Kahan, who interpreted the results, conducted the focus groups, and was a valuable sounding board; and to Roseann Cane and the New York Open Center for providing me with a home for my workshops.

Georgette Kelley's honesty and companionship have been invaluable; Iva Rifkin, Ron Rifkin, Mark Seides, and Joe Warfield have listened to countless accounts of writing and rewriting without ever glazing over; Lita Albuquerque, Allyn Ann McLerie Gaynes and George Gaynes have consistently urged me on.

My gratitude to Richard Parker, whose questions helped me find my writer's voice; and to Barbara Walters, who, through a lifetime of changes, has remained constant.

Robert Gottlieb generously read my first, very long manuscript. His respectful comments silenced my inner critic, and his questions showed me where I needed to go next. He has my thanks, also, for leading me to my agent and friend, Martha Kaplan, whose intelligence, loyalty, and sense of humor have sustained me.

My gifted editor, Carol Southern, enthusiastically supported the manuscript's strengths while gently and unerringly pinpointing its flaws. It is she who is responsible for the book's clarity and coherence, and our collaboration has been an especially happy one for me.

Finally, I wish to acknowledge the people with whom I have worked on this anxiety, especially the former patients and workshop participants who have given me permission to include their material within these pages. It is their courage and tenacity that helped refine the techniques and exercises included in this book, and I am truly grateful to each of them.

Contents

———

Part Two: Resolutions

Love after Love

The time will come
when, with elation,
you will greet yourself arriving
at your own door, in your own mirror,
and each will smile at the other's welcome,

and say, sit here. Eat.
You will love again the stranger who was your self.
Give wine. Give bread. Give back your heart
to itself, to the stranger who has loved you

all your life, whom you ignored
for another, who knows you by heart.
Take down the love letters from the bookshelf,

the photographs, the desperate notes,
peel your own image from the mirror.
Sit. Feast on your life.

—Derek Walcott

Foreword

I HAVE AN EARLY memory of being called on in school to read something aloud to my class. I must have been in third grade, which would make me eight. I was a good reader, but as I heard my name being called, my heart started to pound wildly. My legs trembled as I stood. My face got hot, my mouth dry. I tried to swallow but couldn't. The words seemed to bounce on the pages before me. My mind struggled to concentrate, to complete what should have been an easy task, but what I really wanted to do was disappear.

The incident remains so vivid because it recurred countless times. Always there whenever I was the center of attention, stopping me when I wanted to express myself, this fear was a constant factor in my life.

And now it's gone.

For a long time I thought of what was happening to me as stage fright; most people still use that term when referring to this anxiety. But the degree of fear—panic, really—indicated that this was no ordinary stage fright. Rather, I was suffering from what we now know as performance anxiety—anxiety brought on by being the center of attention.

The difference is important and valuable when it comes to overcoming this fear.

Almost everyone experiences some nervousness at the prospect of speaking in public, but it doesn't escalate into panic. In fact, it soon fades once they are under way, and after a few deep breaths or a positive response from the audience, they are able to enjoy the experience.

But for the millions of people who suffer from performance anxiety, the course is quite different. Their fear begins in anticipation of the event, quickly escalates (often into panic) as they experience themselves watched by others, and does not diminish as they proceed. After the event they are left feeling humiliated and embarrassed. They know that their fear is irrational, and they blame themselves for their inability to control it. And, powerless to change their performance anxiety, they change their lives. They avoid situations where they might call attention to themselves, compromising their careers, limiting their social contacts, and abandoning their talents. In a further attempt to deaden their anxiety, many abuse alcohol and drugs.

The psychological price for this narrowing of experience can be terribly high, forcing many people into loneliness, depression, and despair.

My own performance anxiety went untreated for much of my life. Conventional Freudian analysis never touched it.

Finally, in Jungian analysis, my analyst taught me to dialogue with the people in my dreams. They were an odd collection, running the gamut from bag ladies to grandiose stars. But since they were in my psyche, I had to accept them as part of my psychology, and I needed to learn how they influenced my life. Encouraged by my analyst, I consciously infused them with energy, fleshing them out and interacting with them in my imagination.

And as I did so, my anxiety began to diminish.

Something within me was creating the anxiety, but something in me had brought me to this analyst and was sending me these dreams so I could confront my anxiety—so I could ultimately be free of this anxiety, as I am now.

As you can be, too.

This book is the outgrowth of my work with people who now come to me for treatment of performance anxiety. All of them have learned through this work how to identify and confront the inner sources of their fear. Most of them, armed with this technique, no longer dread their anxiety attacks—they know they can neutralize them before they escalate. And some of these people, having worked for a long enough time, find that performance anxiety is no longer a factor in their lives.

If you are willing to do the work, I believe that you too can diminish—perhaps even eliminate—your performance anxiety.

The technique and exercises are within these pages. Everything else that you need is already within your psyche.

Investigating Severe Stage Fright

————

The symptom is really the effort of the diseased system to cure itself. —C. G. JUNG

"DO YOU SUFFER FROM severe stage fright in business, professional, personal situations?" asked my ad in *The New York Times*. "Yes," replied people from Oregon, Washington, Minnesota, Illinois, Michigan, Maryland, Kentucky, Delaware, New Jersey, Connecticut, and New York. They were men and women from seventeen to seventy-five years of age—actors and musicians, of course, but also doctors, dentists, engineers, lawyers, editors, artists, students, writers, secretaries, executives, stockbrokers, teachers, members of the clergy. Of the 114 people who responded, 42 were interviewed extensively by phone and 13 participated in focus groups. They talked of how their careers and social lives had been limited and their self-esteem diminished by an ongoing and, for some of them, lifelong inability to express themselves in front of others. Many were desperate to overcome their fear.

A picture editor for a magazine spoke of her "paralysis

when I have to give a presentation to a group." An advertising executive told of how "the attacks create such a diversion that all my thoughts go out of whack." A real estate broker said, "I can't ever take any job where I have to talk in public."

Some are sleepless before a presentation; some overeat. Some become "obsessive," overpreparing, though it doesn't do any good. A salesman told us, "I can stay up all night and go over the figures a hundred times and have them memorized cold, and then completely flub it up. If I'm addressing a group, I'm blank. The memory just goes out the window."

"I have more of a problem in one-on-one situations," said an engineer. "It's a matter of how much power the person seems to have to change my situation. Especially in interviews. My chest starts to tighten on the way there, and I start hyperventilating. By the time I get there, I'm soaked with perspiration. I get so discombobulated that I give very short, abrupt, evasive answers, and all I want to do is get out of there."

A lawyer was one of many who regularly uses alcohol for his panic attacks. He talked of having to get "boozed up" to go to court. Others spoke of medication—beta-blockers, Inderal, Xanax, Valium. Medication was unreliable or ineffective for some, too sedating for others, contraindicated for those with histories of addiction.

But their anxiety was not limited to work-related situations. Many said it permeated their personal lives as well.

"I compete in tennis and I also get these same feelings before every match," said a teacher. "I'm sick to my stomach, I feel very numb, my palms are very sweaty, I'm light-headed. The more important the match, the more the palpitations. And if I realize I'm winning, it gets worse—until I lose."

A retired broker spoke of his need to "get drunk to deliver a eulogy at a very good friend's funeral." A graduate student talked of hiding in the ladies' room so she wouldn't have to deliver a toast at her best friend's wedding. "I hate going to parties," said a social worker. An architect called herself a "wallflower." A doctor said that to compensate for how he feels socially, he "comes on too strong."

All talked of their physical symptoms—of nausea and "heaving," blushing, perspiring, pounding in the ears, difficulty in breathing or in focusing eyesight or attention, feeling dizzy or faint, inability to speak, shaking hands, excessive need to urinate—of the fear they would "die," and feelings they had of "falling apart," of "freezing up." One had been diagnosed incorrectly in high school as suffering from Epstein-Barr—a chronic fatigue syndrome. A writer talked of his "paralysis" each time he approached his word processor. An actor said that "waiting in the wings, I almost get diarrhea and gag to the point of nearly vomiting. I always swear to myself that this is the last time I'll work on stage."

A museum director was one of several who described her experience of depersonalization. "I was there standing, talking, but at the same time I felt outside of my body, up in the air observing myself." The attacks were described as "humiliating," "embarrassing," "overwhelming," "devastating," "shattering," "crippling," "limiting," "terrifying," "tormenting."

Our oldest respondent, a seventy-five-year-old lawyer, said, "I've had this all my life. I never thought of it as stage fright until I saw the ad. I said, 'Oh, my God, maybe that's what it is.' It gave me some answers, something to pin it on. I've always thought, I'm just screwing up again, I'm not sharp enough to deal with the questions, I have to fake it. I don't think anybody sees how upset I am. They just think I'm dumb. All I'm thinking is, How fast can I sit down? How can I not be too humiliated doing it? . . . I've got a case now which may go to the Supreme Court of the United States. It's an honor, but it's something that I'm just not going to do. I'll get another attorney to argue. I couldn't take the chance of blowing it.''

Our youngest respondent, a seventeen-year-old college student, said, ''I wish I didn't have to be like this all my life. You know you could do it as well as other people, and that hurts you.''

You know you could do it as well as other people, but no matter what you do or how hard you try, you can't.

And you can't explain to people who don't suffer from performance anxiety that what they experience with their fear and what you experience with yours is as different as night from day.

If the person suffering this way is your spouse, or your child, or your friend, it is difficult for you to understand why they are so frightened, and it is impossible for you to help them.

Chances are you do know someone with this degree of stage fright, though the shame associated with this disorder causes many sufferers to go to great lengths to hide it. According to a major 1993 study by Bruskin/Goldring Research, what they referred to as ''stage fright'' affects 50 percent (93 million) of adults in America; 19 percent (18 million people) report it to be ''a moderate or severe and/or frequent source of disruption.'' Of this group, 13 percent (11.9 million people) say it is ''always lurking in the background.'' Their responses, like those of many who answered my ad, suggest that they suffer from performance anxiety.

Performance anxiety is still a relatively unknown term, but even more confusing is the fact that this anxiety disorder has been categorized and investigated by the medical establishment as "social phobia."

Concerned that people might not identify their fear as either performance anxiety or social phobia, I asked about "severe stage fright" in both my ad and my research. My instinct was right. All the respondents who were asked said that they would not have recognized or responded to the other terms. (For this reason I have also used *stage fright* in the title of this book.)

I was not surprised by their response. It wasn't until 1985 that the first in-depth studies of this group of anxiety disorders appeared in the professional literature. Today, the *Bulletin of the Menninger Clinic* calls social phobia "underrecognized and thus undertreated," and contributors to the *Bulletin* confirm that it is "the most common anxiety disorder" in the country . . . "responsible for larger economic loss, greater interpersonal disruption, and deeper personal pain than can be easily measured by modern accounting methods."

DO YOU SUFFER FROM PERFORMANCE ANXIETY?

Here's how you can tell.
More often than not:

1. Does the thought of publicly stating your opinions fill you with dread?
2. If forced to make a speech of public statement, do you

experience ongoing symptoms of anxiety, such as heart pounding, shortness of breath, excessive perspiration, trembling limbs, inability to think? Do you blush, stammer, feel stupid?

3. Do you anticipate negative evaluation by others, especially those in authority?

4. Does an invitation to a party bring you as much anxiety as pleasure?

5. Does being observed by others make you feel terribly anxious?

6. Do you think of yourself as extremely shy or self-conscious?

7. Are you afraid of making a fool of yourself?

8. Do you fear being humiliated?

9. Would you find the exposure of these fears humiliating?

10. Have you made, and do you continue to make, professional and social choices that are severely limited by these fears?

11. Moreover, do you recognize that your fears are irrational and berate yourself for having them?

If most of your answers are "yes," don't despair. You don't have to spend the rest of your life with this suffering. You have a treatable anxiety disorder.

My technique for the treatment of performance anxiety evolved from my own analytic work and my subsequent work with some of the patients who had come to me for Jungian analysis. Though performance anxiety was not the stated reason for their having sought treatment—it rarely is—performance anxiety emerged as a central ongoing problem in their lives.

Analysis of their dreams and fantasies revealed critical, perfectionistic, belittling parts of the psyche, always warning of dire consequences, sabotaging each one's ability to risk being seen and heard.

They began to realize (as I had before them) that their anxiety attacks were the result of a battle between parts of the psyche—the part that wanted to express itself versus a terrorizing part (or parts) determined to silence them. Their anxiety, then, contrary to the way in which *they* perceived it, was about the judgments not of an outer "audience," but rather of an inner one.

Most often this sabotaging part manifested as an inner "voice," which, when listened to carefully, evoked memories of people and occurrences in childhood. (In fact, most professionals believe that performance anxiety has its roots in childhood experience.)

Many of these people had histories of emotional and/or physical abuse, receiving repeated messages of their lack of value from a parent or other important caretaker. These negative judgments were replayed mentally each time they displayed themselves, voiced their ideas, or expressed their talents.

But parental abuse was not the only cause of performance anxiety.

Some people had been raised by mothers whose chronic depression made them incapable of providing their children with a basic sense of security. These people suffered from a variety of adjustment disorders—low self-esteem and anxiety being only two of them. Some had come from anxiety-filled homes, where their parents' fear of negative judgments from others had caused them to be perfectionistic and overly controlling with their children. For these people, perfectionism and anxiety had become a way of life, both a learned response and the emotional link to their families.

Some had been pulled between loving but poorly matched parents, unconsciously assuming responsibility for the emptiness in Mom or Dad. These people had become the carriers of their parents' unlived lives, unconsciously rejecting their own truth in trying to fulfill their parents' dreams.

And for some people, childhood security had been fractured by the early loss of a loved one or an invasive medical procedure.

The ability of these patients to gain insight into the roots of their fear was valuable, but it was only a beginning; intellectual awareness did not go far enough. Even reexperiencing their feelings in relation to what may have been trauma had little or no effect on their performance anxiety.

What *was* effective for them, and later for other patients and workshop participants, was active engagement with their own inner voices and the images that accompanied them—in other words, encounters with the imaginary people who are the personified energy in the unconscious.

Using a combination of acting exercises and psychological techniques, each person was helped to confront and do battle with his or her internal tormentors. In treatment they were encouraged literally to stand up and talk back and/or physically act out feelings toward these powerful adversarial inner voices, often for the first time. They learned, through these repeated confrontations, that by speaking out, they were changing their relationship to their fear. The result of this repeated work was that symptoms were greatly diminished—and, for some, eliminated entirely.

People who have worked on their performance anxiety in this way have also said that they experience a more widespread change. They have reported new feelings of aliveness in their bodies, new physical and emotional freedom, and (for some) newly realized connection with a rich inner source of which they were previously unaware.

What follows is a close look at performance anxiety: profiles of three people who suffered from this disorder, excerpts from a short-term workshop, and most important, step-by-step instructions to help you overcome your anxiety as my patients and workshop participants have overcome theirs.

Some of you reading this book may have had little or no experience with psychology. If that is so, it may be hard for you to accept ideas that may make little sense to you, theories that may be foreign to your nature.

I believe that if you are willing to stay with this material, you will become convinced of the reality of an inner world—the unconscious—which works in concert with the outer one. Whether or not we believe in this other dimension, we are influenced by it. When accepted and accessed, it can be the source of our deepest support. My approach to this inner world is through the teachings of C. G. Jung.

Dr. Jung was a pioneer in depth psychology. A deeply spiritual man, he believed that each of us has a specific life to live and that everything that comes into our lives is deliberately intended by a higher power for our growth and development. To put it another way, everything with which we are confronted has meaning related to our wholeness.

But the communication, coming from the unconscious, appears in symbolic language and is, therefore, not readily understood.

To learn the meaning of our performance anxiety we must learn to communicate with the unconscious.

We do this when we value and explore our dreams and fantasies and the feelings and symptoms in our bodies. This allows us to make conscious the underlying dynamics that make us feel and react the way we do.

But we cannot stop there. Insight without action is valueless. In order to lessen the impact of our fear, we must use what we have learned to do battle with the energy underlying our performance anxiety, the energy within ourselves that sabotages us.

If you will gather your courage, I will help you confront your anxiety. In its energy are precious pieces of your own personality, pieces of yourself that have been in hiding for a long time. Allow these parts of yourself into consciousness and they will broaden your life. You will become more authentic, more complete, more the person you were born to be.

And you will be less afraid.

PART ONE

Explorations

Stage Fright: Three Profiles

———

*When the ego has been made a ''seat of anxiety,''
someone is running away from himself and will not
admit it.*
                                            —C. G. JUNG

EACH OF US IS born with the potential for the unfolding of
our true self. When we deviate from this truth, we are
interfering with the intention of something far greater than
we are—call it nature or a higher power—and as a result, we
develop discomfort in our bodies and psyches. Therefore,
our anxiety symptoms may be regarded as meaningful communication from a powerful force within us that wants us to
be ourselves.

What is being communicated by our performance anxiety?
   The energy in our overwhelming fear indicates that something of importance is at issue here; something that runs
counter to our conscious position is struggling to make itself
known.
   Rather than choosing to run away from our anxiety, as
we do when we deny, shut down, or anesthetize, we must
enter into a new relationship with it. We must confront our

anxiety so that we may truly be seen and heard—so that our true self may manifest in its fullness in reality.

The following three profiles, one constructed from writings, two that came from my practice, offer examinations of performance anxiety and suggest what is necessary for this confrontation.

Laurence Olivier

[Stage fright] is an animal, a monster which hides in its foul corner without revealing itself, but you know that it is there and that it may come forward at any moment.
—L. OLIVIER, ON ACTING

Laurence Olivier is thought by some to have been the greatest actor of our time. But this didn't protect him from panic attacks on stage.

In his autobiography he writes that his performance in *The Master Builder* marked "the beginning of the terrors." He was then fifty-seven years old. In fact, what he calls "the terrors" began when he was thirteen.

The onset of his most debilitating panic attacks, which were to last unabated for five and a half years and throughout countless performances, struck a year after his triumphant opening as the first director of the National Theater at the Old Vic in London. He had decided, in celebration of his new appointment, that he should "condemn" himself to "a year of abstinence" from the alcohol he enjoyed so often and in such abundance. He had been an actor and a drinker for almost fifty years.

It certainly seems possible that it was in part the loss of

this habitual way of deadening his feelings that allowed his anxiety to break through on stage. But Olivier attributed his panic symptoms to "some overblown claim to pride in myself [that] would be bound to find the punishment that it deserved." Punishment had long been a factor in his life.

The third child in a clergyman's family, Olivier writes in his autobiography of his perception of the "disgust" his father felt on his first view of him.

My father . . . couldn't see the slightest purpose in my existence. Everything about me irritated him.

A child sees itself as it is seen by its parents; rejection by a parent becomes internalized and grows into self-rejection. In later years Olivier would repeatedly attribute what he called his stage fright to some failure in himself.

He continues:

When did I ever have the guts to confront my father about anything, to tell him his attitudes were stupid, childish, wrong, sometimes close to being wicked in their dangerous prejudices and ignorance?

He never did. But how he idolized his mother! It was she who would happily sit as his audience during his many eager childhood attempts at putting on shows.

My heaven, my hope, my entire world, my own worshiped Mummy . . . lovely . . . gifted with a delightful wit and serenely high spirits.

She had three children under the age of five when he was born, her own "inheritance" was "modest" and her husband's stipend "meager." Olivier writes, understandably, that she was "greatly overstressed." She died when he was twelve, and he never got over the loss. He talks of the "undisguisedly frank favoritism of my mother for her Baby," and that "I alone needed her special protection." (Perhaps this was because, according to his sister, it was Larry who was singled out for his father's wrath.)

Yet it was Olivier's mother who administered repeated severe spankings to "her Baby."

> [My] second earliest memory was of a first spanking . . . when I was three. [From ages five to nine:] My Mummy had, more often than it pleases me to remember, to quell the natural anguish which she suffered at what was to her the dreaded prospect of spanking me for one inveterate and seemingly irresistible sin, that of lying. It was apparently impossible for me to resist this temptation. It was a compulsion in me. . . .

He goes on to justify her behavior:

> I felt sure in my heart, and still do, that she would not risk giving his [her husband's] displeasure full rein in case he did not know when to stop. He had been a schoolmaster with a lasting reputation for severity before taking Holy Orders. How much the nobler, then, my mother's voluntary self-punishment. . . .

Later, he writes:

After three or four years of the monotonous exchange of sin and punishment, it eventually pierced my sluggish little brain that this operation really did hurt her more than it hurt me. I noticed at last while I was removing the necessary garments that she was in a state of high distress. . . . I thereupon resolved that she should never again be made to suffer in this way . . . so my habit of lying ceased . . . for a time, anyway.

He was silent before his father's rejection and in total denial of his reactions to his mother's cruelty.

Where were his true feelings about these parents whose love he was dependent upon? I believe they were feeding his performance anxiety and erupting in panic.

His first recorded panic attack on stage occurred a year after his mother died. It was she who trained him "with utmost diligence, playing for me on her piano . . . nursing a private ambition" that he join the choir of All Saints Church.

During what he knew would be his final performance as soloist with that choir, he suffered this "treacherous phenomenon." Of that first attack he writes:

My breath left my body and could not be retrieved; my throat closed up and I was forced to stop. . . .

Sixty-one years later, on writing this book, he said:

These crises were unpredictably sporadic and have been a nightmare to me all my life in public appearances.

His accounts of these panic attacks are laced through his writings. From *On Acting:*

[It] is always waiting outside the door, any door, waiting to get you. You either battle or walk away. . . . Suddenly there he is: the bogeyman comes along and tries to rob you of your living. He can come at any time, in any form. The dark shadow of fear. . . . Just when you think you've conquered it, there it is sitting at the end of the bed grinning at you.

His solution at that time?

I have given instructions to the other actors not to look me in the eyes. My company—what a thing to do to them. But I had to. The one thing an actor must do is look his fellow actor in the eyes, and I have asked my fellow players not to. . . . For some reason this made me feel that there was not quite so much loaded against me.

Here is an outgrowth of Olivier's repeated spankings. In our culture we lower our eyes, avert our gaze, when we are ashamed; shame, a central element in performance anxiety, is a by-product of corporal punishment.

But he had also begged the actor playing Iago (in *Othello*) to be visible to him at all times, even when offstage, "since I feared I might not be able to stay there in front of the audience by myself."

For most people with performance anxiety, the escalation to panic occurs when they become aware of being watched. Then they, too, like Olivier, want to run away, even if they are in the middle of a presentation.

Olivier had a deep aversion to introspection and psychoanalysis and so implies that he never attempted to treat his panic.

He does not see the possibility that his ongoing use of alcohol was an attempt at self-medication. And though he suggests that the attacks just wore themselves out, his biographer, Donald Spoto, writes that he finally resorted to the use of Valium to control his terror.

His professed "recovery" from "stage fright" was marked by the onset of years of serious and painful illnesses, among them prostate cancer, repeated pneumonias, thrombosis of his right leg, and urinary problems that required what he identifies as "the most serious surgery" and which would plague him for the rest of his life. While I do not suggest that we "create" our illnesses, the body and psyche are interwoven and cannot be separated, and when we don't deal with psychological pain it will find expression in the body. It is fair to wonder how much Olivier's denial of psychological pain predisposed him to his physical emergencies.

The medical crises were in addition to his excessive use of alcohol and his many ongoing medical problems, including intermittent suicidal depression, gout, and severe hemorrhoids. One of his final illnesses was a disease called acute dermatomyositis, a grave connective tissue disease, which, in addition to causing dull pain throughout his body, acute dryness of the skin, facial swelling so severe that his eyes all but disappeared, and atrophy and loss of muscle use, made any touch extremely painful.

What irony there is in this, the pain of any touch.

In the following excerpt from *On Acting* Olivier writes about the relation of the actor to the audience:

> *When the actor is on stage, it is he and he alone who drives the moment. The audience have no choice but to*

remain in his faith or leave. That's the true excitement, the real magic of the profession. The actor on stage is all-powerful, for once the curtain rises, he is in control. . . .

But later in this same section he writes:

Without them you do not exist. Without them you are a man alone in a room with memories and a mirror. Without them you are nothing.

What a testament it is to the scope of his talent that he was able to elevate and illuminate the human condition for the rest of us, while remaining helpless and in flight before his own inner demons.

Marcy

As I walked forward I felt very far away and sort of dead. . . . I couldn't breathe. I couldn't see through the light. I couldn't swallow. I barely could talk. . . . I knew it would be the same next time.

Marcy was forty-four at the time she sought treatment for depression. She worked as a music teacher at a private school, grateful to have a job in which she dealt primarily with children. But the job also required her to have routine meetings with parents and to play for them during school musicales, and these occasions were a nightmare of anxiety for her. In addition, she suffered greatly during the weekly staff meetings. Here she was mute with dread, unable to voice her opinions, certain that everyone would find her ideas "stupid," convinced that she would be humiliated.

Her dream, long since abandoned, had been to sing in musical theater, but despite many years of training and encouragement from others, she was crippled with fear whenever she sang in public. At such times, hardly able to get into her breath, she would try to push her own light lyric soprano voice, finding it "too small," having early been impressed by Ethel Merman, whose powerhouse persona and brassy sound she had wanted to emulate.

Singing in private was a different matter. When singing alone, she would feel "full of joy" and free of critical self-judgments. At these times her singing came from something deep inside her; it was the expression of her true self.

Her last singing attempt in public had been several years before we began our work, at a recital at her singing teacher's studio. She had agreed at the last minute to take the place of another student who was suddenly unable to appear. It had happened so close to the recital that she hadn't been able to do her usual obsessing in anticipation of singing in public. She thought maybe she could just get away with it. She recalled:

I was to walk up to the piano and explain that I was not the person listed on the program and announce what I would sing. My cue came and as I walked forward I felt very far away and sort of dead. I got to the piano and was struck dumb by the spotlight. It hadn't been there during rehearsal. I couldn't breathe. I couldn't see through the light. I couldn't swallow. I barely could talk. I don't know how I got through the song, but it wasn't any good. My teacher said afterward, "Well, now you've done it and it won't ever be that bad again," but I knew he was wrong. I knew it would be the same next time. It was like being pinned in a searchlight by the Gestapo, knowing that in the next moment their machine guns would kill me.

This suggested to me that in her childhood when Marcy had tried to express herself, she had felt mercilessly shot down as the Nazis had shot down their victims. But, because it was her fantasy, it also suggested an aspect of herself of which she was unconscious at that time—the "Nazi" part of her own personality, the part that wanted to kill her freedom to express herself.

Here are the important elements in her history:

Marcy was raised in New England. There was no religious practice in the family; money was the family's god, so the highest value was accorded to material things. This left her with no conscious access to her own inner life.

Today her mother will say, with pride, "You were the smartest child there ever was; you could recite 'The Night Before Christmas' when you were only four," but Marcy doesn't remember this. What she does remember was being scolded repeatedly for "showing off," being told she was "too smart" for her own good and "no one will ever like you." Like Olivier, she was caught in a double bind, both encouraged and punished by her mother for similar behavior.

There were also penetrating, verbal attacks directed at her, seemingly out of nowhere, the result of her mother's frequent rages. Now she believes that her mother was jealous of her because she was "Daddy's favorite girl."

When she was four a confluence of factors occurred that she later came to recognize as traumatic. Her mother's father, the patriarch of the family, whose loving smile Marcy still remembers, suddenly died. His death, Marcy feels, shattered her security. Soon after, her only sibling, a brother who was named for the dead grandfather, was born.

With the arrival of the new baby, Marcy found that her mother was unavailable. In her mother's stead was a new nursemaid into whose exclusive care the child was given. She was a newly arrived immigrant, young and very homesick, deeply drawn to the new baby as if he were her own, and unresponsive to Marcy. Now there were two rejecting "mothers."

Her father, who worked on the road as a salesman, was away much of the time. He was never able to satisfy his wife's demands for material and social advancement, but for Marcy, his return home would mean that there was warmth in the house. She felt loved by him, and being wary of her mother's wrath, she found that her most precious times, her only times of happiness in childhood, were when she and her father were alone together. He became the center of her life, and she would do anything to please him. For his part, the unconditional love he received from his daughter provided a gratifying contrast to the unrelenting demands of his wife.

Her earliest memory of tension around singing was due to his reaction.

When she was ten, the family was visiting a resort, and one morning, drawn by the sound of a piano, she had sung with the pianist. She remembers the man excitedly asking her to sing that night in a kiddie show for the grown-ups. Happily she told her parents. To her astonishment, her father became "furious" and "forbade" her to sing. He never explained why, but she thought it meant that her singing wasn't good enough and that he was afraid she would embarrass him. She did not sing with the other children that night.

Some years later when she said she wanted to be a singer, he replied that anyone who was a singer was a "whore." By the time she began to go on dates, her perception of him as warm and loving had changed, for he, like her mother, had become critical and full of anger.

In our early analytic work, Marcy radiated controlled anxiety. Her eyes were in constant motion as she flitted from topic to topic in an "entertaining" way. This was her usual "social" behavior. Since the only time she received attention or approval from her mother was when she was entertaining or "beautiful," she could not afford to be "ordinary." Love and approval from her father were also conditional—she would be loved only on the condition that she stay his adoring little girl. Thus, to be pleasing rather than to be genuine became her goal.

The price was the hiding of her true responses and feelings—that is, her true self—and the assumption of an artificial personality—a false self. It is possible that her true self—the experience of herself as she sang—was also protected from criticism by her performance anxiety.

In our sessions, Marcy habitually tried to please me and watched for signs and signals that she was succeeding in doing so. As she grew to trust me and this pattern of behavior became conscious, she was able sometimes to let down the facade she usually exhibited and allow her genuineness to come through. At these times she dropped her bright outer-directed mask and became intelligent and thoughtful. Now she was inner directed, reflecting on herself rather than being a reflection of others.

———

There was another major issue that I knew was related to her anxiety—her mother's verbal assaults. But it took quite some time before Marcy could deal with them.

When I had first tried to examine her feelings around this issue, she dismissed my questions, saying merely that she had gotten used to it. Ultimately she was able to admit to feeling "very ugly." "I hate that little girl, snotty and always in trouble," she said with passion.

Then, realizing I was watching her, she cried:

> *Don't look at me. I'm too ashamed. I can't stand to have you see me. Don't be sympathetic. I don't want it. It makes me more pitiful, and I can't stand it. I hate that little girl.*

It was not until she had expressed these feelings to me that she knew this was how she felt about herself. She was shocked by her shame and self-hatred.

She was beginning to learn that in having been verbally abused, she had internalized her mother's hatred. Now some part of her psyche behaved toward herself in the same abusive way. By way of compensation, everything she did had to be "perfect."

This opened the way for a new relationship toward the child she had been—the child who was still alive within her psyche. In fantasy we returned to the scenes of her childhood punishments many times. Initially she would merely objectively observe herself as the unhappy child she had been. But new, tender feelings began to grow for the child, and she was no longer able to keep a cool distance from her. She would invite the child onto her lap and hold her as she wept; soon they would weep together. Ultimately her fantasies enlarged to include her angry assaulting mother, and she was able to confront her, voicing the thoughts and feelings that the child had been too frightened and powerless to express. Through these repeated confrontations, she diminished her mother's belittling internalized voice, and her anxiety began to lighten.

In another fantasy one day, Marcy allowed herself to go back twenty years to a singing audition. She had wanted the job very much, she thought, and had prepared diligently. As she took herself through the audition, in the fantasy/memory her voice was warmed up, open and free. The sound and sensation pleased her, and her nerves were under control. But as she acknowledged the pleasure and freedom in her singing, as she realized that she was doing well enough to get the job, she began to panic and saw herself backing away. This was a pivotal realization. Now she saw that part of her had not wanted the jobs for which she had worked so hard.

She said:

> *I always had fantasies of being a great star, of having them finally say how wonderful and special I was. But I see that getting the job, being a singer, being what I wanted, would have meant the end of my relationship with my parents. I wouldn't any longer be connected to them. I couldn't dare that. I wanted to stay in the safe lonely hell of my childhood. It was all I had.*

Her performance anxiety, then, had served a purpose. It had kept her attached to her parents.

Ultimately Marcy was able to acknowledge that acquiring her parents' love and approval had been the driving—and limiting—force of her life. She came to realize that her parents' inability to give her what she needed was due to something in their own histories and natures, not because of some deficit in herself. By accepting this truth, she could move away from the past.

By the end of our work together, Marcy's depression was gone and her anxiety had faded. Freed from her mother's internalized negativity, she no longer perceived her colleagues as wanting to find a flaw in her every idea. She was also able to share the students' excitement when parents attended the recitals, playing for them with pleasure, enjoying her own musical talent and happily accepting their applause, no longer plagued by the need to be "perfect."

Sometime after we terminated our work together, Marcy wrote to tell me that she had started singing again. She had gone back to her old teacher and then auditioned successfully for a local choir, with some nervousness but not the old crippling panic. This is not the fulfillment of her fantasy to sing a leading part on Broadway, but it is giving her great pleasure. Her singing is no longer a vehicle for imagined power—she doesn't need to be a "star"—but, rather, singing is a way of expressing her deepest nature. She says her voice is more open than before, more naturally powerful than it was when she had pushed it to sound like Ethel Merman. Now she is able to sing for others the way she has always sung for herself.

Anne

I'll do practically anything to get myself out of presentations. If I feel the audience is judgmental or critical or

*uninterested in what I have to say, I just fall apart. So
now I take medication when I know I have to present
something to a client. But it doesn't always work.*

Anne, forty-seven, an account executive at a well-known
advertising agency, had been assigned to an important new
account. The week before she came for treatment, she had
frozen during a presentation for her new client, as she had
several times before under similar circumstances. A colleague of Anne's, with whom I had worked, identified her
problem as performance anxiety and had referred her to me.

Anne felt that her ideas for this account were exciting,
but, as always, presenting them filled her with dread. She
had a background of analytic work and had used medication
to control her panic for years. Mostly it worked, but sometimes it made her thinking "muddy." This time it had failed
and the panic had broken through. Now she didn't trust the
medication. At the meeting she had blamed her difficulty on
flu and fever and another member of her team had taken
over for her. But this had happened too many times. She
was afraid she might lose the account and perhaps her job as
well. When she came to see me, she was desperate.

Our agreed-upon goal was to get her through her next
presentation the following month.

We had a total of four sessions over a five-week period.
After the third session she was able to do the presentation
without medication and without panic.

During our first hour I asked her to explain the circumstances triggering her attacks and to describe her physical
symptoms during the attacks as fully as possible. It was
difficult for her to stay with her symptoms; she preferred

immediately to go into family history. In describing herself, she used the words "I was exposed . . . I am a sham." Her father was overtly sexual with her, on the one hand, and belittling ("scapegoated me") on the other. Her mother was "a zero." Anne's rage and hatred were palpable.

Her first therapy was in her early twenties. In her early forties she was put on medication for depression, and this she still continued to take intermittently.

She said, "I'm so tired of walking around with this. It's as if I've been hanging on to the edge of a cliff and I have to let go."

I asked that she bring some of the presentation to the next week's session. We would use her material to elicit her anxiety.

By the end of our first session, I believed that if Anne could express her feelings of hatred and rage to her parents now—as she had been unable to do in childhood—she would get some relief from her symptoms. We would set up imaginary confrontations during her subsequent sessions.

She called before each session either to confirm or clarify the time of our meeting. It felt as if she were asking, "Are you there for me? Are you expecting me?" I did not analyze her calls but merely confirmed our appointments.

During the second session she said:

I'm so nervous about presenting this. I'm afraid they won't be able to hear me. Most of the time when I think about it I want to cry. . . . What really went on that I should think so poorly of myself? It's as if I'm transparent. Not solid.

I guided her in a relaxation exercise, asking her to close her eyes and to concentrate first on her toes, then the arches of her feet, then her heels, then ankles, and so on, until, very slowly, methodically, we had covered her body with our attention. All the while she was encouraged to allow tension to let go whenever she found it in that place in her body. After we had completed this process, I directed her to concentrate on her breathing, to just watch it come and go. Thoughts, when they came, were to be observed and released, and concentration was to be redirected back to the body or the breathing—whatever we were working on at the moment of intrusion of the thought. By the time she completed the relaxation exercise, she was in a meditative state, and the unconscious was more available. She was then directed to allow her imagination to lead her wherever it wished.

What she "saw" was herself as a child. I asked her to "become" the little Anne and to speak to me.

ANNE: I feel very little. Just depressed.

I: What else are you feeling?

ANNE: It's anger. This is something that's been with me for a long time.

I instructed her to let her body do whatever it wanted and, still with her eyes closed, she began to make movements with her arm, which I asked her to exaggerate. She did so repeatedly and fiercely.

ANNE: I want to stab someone.

I: What is in your hand?

ANNE: I have an imaginary knife.

I: Let it be real.

ANNE: It's not so big, but it's sharp.

I asked her to stand, and she did so. Without my prompting, she made vigorous stabbing motions.

ANNE: I'm stabbing somebody's stomach . . . my father's.

Over and over she was stabbing the air with her "knife," grunting from the effort, following my instruction that she allow whatever sound wanted to accompany her actions.

Suddenly she opened her eyes and smiled.

ANNE: I'm getting it out.

I: Who is the most frightening person in the world for you to present your work to?

She began to cry.

I: Who is it?

More tears.

ANNE: I don't know.

I: Who is it?

ANNE: My father.

She sobbed.

I pulled an empty chair next to me, saying this was her father, and asked her to present her work to us, to allow the fear to come up and tell me about it. She began to do so. She felt the fear in her chest, in her throat. I asked her to let out what she felt there and to talk to her "father." Quietly she began:

> *I wish you'd been more capable as a parent. I wish your craziness hadn't spilled out onto my brother and me.*

I handed her an encounter bat, a long-handled, heavily padded batlike device used by some therapists as a physical aid to help patients express feelings. Armed with this, hefting it, she began to let go. She said:

Probably the first time you did anything to me was when Nana got sick and Mother had to go to her. I was very young. She said I wasn't the same when she came back. . . . I remember one time when you made me take my panties down in front of the maid and made her watch while you spanked me—to humiliate me. And you got some kick out of it. (She was now pounding the chair.) . . . It feels like everybody is going to be bored and I'm not going to hold their attention. Maybe I don't want it. Because then I wouldn't be exposed. . . . I used to cry in my room for hours and you'd let me be in there for two or three hours and then you'd come into my room and rub my stomach.

Again she had used the word "exposed" as she had in an earlier session. Now I realized that it related to her taking her panties down for the spankings. Olivier's punishment and shame could be seen now in Anne's history as well.

And again there is the double bind for the child—abuse and then "comfort" by the abuser. How confusing for the child to have the parent be so hating and so "loving." The sadism and the sexual overtones of Anne's father's are unmistakable.

Anne went back to doing her presentation. Intermittently, whenever she felt the need to strike her "father," to express her anger, she hit the empty chair with the bat. In that manner she presented her work in my office.

Afterward she said, "It feels good to do that." As she left, she said that next week she would like to deal with her mother.

At the onset of the third session she told me of her experience after she had left our second session, saying she had never felt such a freedom, a lightness. She said she was ready to present her work the next day, that after the last session she had become aware—

—how I'm pushed down everywhere. I'm very aware of fear of people. I know I merge too fast with people. Like I don't know where they leave off and I begin. I tire easily around people and have to get off and be by myself.

I explained that her fatigue might be due to her hypervigilance—common self-protective behavior in people who have been abused. I told her that people who have been physically abused will try to "leave" the site of their pain and often feel as if they were outside of their bodies. This can make them feel porous and ungrounded.

I also told her that unexpressed rage can turn back and attack the body as physical illness and/or depression. (I learned in the next session that in addition to depression, she had had cancer some years before.)

I asked her to stand and make her presentation, again pulling an empty chair into the center of the room. "Who is it going to be today?" I asked.

ANNE: (Touching her waist) I guess my father. It's going up to my throat and my chest. I feel very hopeless. It's a lot of rage. I always want to strike out when I feel this way. (She hit the couch with the encounter bat.) That's my father. It feels like I could throw up. It's pain. It could be an ulcer.

I: Make the sound of how it feels.

ANNE: (She did so and began pounding with her fists.) I want to rip him up. I want to tie him up. I want to kill him. "You're so selfish. So self-centered. You really used me. You used my brother. You used my mother, and she was too weak to deal with you or to protect us."

I: What about her?

ANNE: My mother held everything in. Then she would let out her anger. She'd yell at us. "Anne, your hair's a mess."

I: Who is in the chair?

ANNE: (Slowly) I guess it's my mother. She never listened to us. It feels horrible. . . . I feel like I don't count. I'm not even a person. I think she's so—I hate her. I hate her today. . . . (To the empty chair) You're such a bitch. You take everything out on me. You take care of my brother. Only he counts. . . .

The whole hour became a monologue of hatred and pain. Resting toward the end of the session, she said, "I think I can do this now."

The fourth and final session was two weeks after the third. In the interim she had done her presentation. She was radiant when she arrived. In a rush she said:

I did fine. I thought of you. I wanted to stay in touch with the anger. I thought my voice would project more. At first I was really afraid to look up. So I read and concentrated on my voice. My legs weren't shaky. I became focused on what I was doing. I looked at the clients.

I feel that now I have a different experience in my life. I now have a sense of myself getting up and being able to talk without getting a shot or popping a pill and I've

*never had it before. I've lived so much of my life trying
to work around being scared.*

I had represented our work not as a "cure," but rather as
a way of confronting what was fueling Anne's panic attacks.
Indeed, I made it clear during the last session that for the
"healing" to be reliable, confrontation with the parts of
herself responsible for her performance anxiety would have
to be engaged in repeatedly.

When she called me four months later for an unrelated
problem, Anne had remained symptom-free and was, to her
surprise, looking forward to her next presentation the following week.

The Dynamics of Performance Anxiety

[The] young, growing part of the personality, if prevented from living or kept in check, generates fear. . . .
—C. G. JUNG

NO ONE IS BORN afraid of being seen and heard. Therefore, something must have happened to those of us who suffer from performance anxiety to convince us that being the center of attention would bring us psychological and/or physical pain. And for virtually all the people with whom I have worked on this anxiety, the expectation of pain was ultimately traceable to interactions with parents—both their actual behavior and their unspoken messages.

That is not to say the only cause of anxiety in children is parental influence. It is not. (The loss of a loved one or an invasive medical procedure are but two examples of trauma that can deeply undermine a child's basic sense of security.) But when a child's anxiety expresses itself in the consistent terror of being seen and heard, overt or covert parental (or caretaker) involvement appears always to have been present.

In childhood we internalize our parents' attitudes about

us, and their view of us—or what we perceive to be their view—provides the cornerstone for how we see ourselves. If our parents encourage us to develop in ways that are natural to us, we grow up feeling that we're pretty much all right the way we are. If they do not, we assume that there is something wrong with us—something that we had better change or hide. (It would be too frightening to think that there is something wrong with *them*.) We split off our true self and live out of a false identity, trying to appear as if we were what we think they want us to be. Blaming ourselves for their lack of validation, we repeat and repeat our early adaptation of trying to please so we will not be abandoned. We replay the same dynamic with teachers and bosses, partners and lovers, with everyone upon whom we project parental authority. Or we create it with our children by unconsciously believing that if we love them enough, if we are "perfect" parents, they will give us the love and approval we never had. Thus their lives, too, become compromised as they are coerced into carrying our need for love and approval.

The emptiness and anxiety that we experience long after childhood is the legacy of our need to deny our authenticity. It is a high price to pay for the illusion of safety, but it was intuited by us as necessary for both physical and psychological survival. In other words, through this assumption of a false self, we did more than merely ensure that our physical needs would be met. At a time when we were unable to support or protect ourselves in any other way, we also found a means to defend our true self by keeping it hidden.

In addition, if parents are habitually dismissive and rejecting, critical and perfectionistic, and most particularly when they are verbally and/or physically abusive to us or a sibling, we become conditioned by their treatment to dismiss, reject, belittle, punish, and abuse the young, instinctual parts of ourselves, and we do so. Genuine feelings and behavior that were unacceptable to our parents are now experienced with anxiety or are repressed and pushed out of consciousness. Authentic reactions and impulses are subjected to a careful, sometimes conscious but most often unconscious, screening process lest they erupt and cause us further pain. *Performance* then, rather than genuine being, becomes the child's—and later the adult's—way of life.

Further, when children are repeatedly physically punished and/or verbally attacked and belittled by their parents, deep emotional scars remain in the psyche long after the physical pain has gone. In addition to anxiety, these may be feelings of hatred, rage, terror, humiliation, shame, and helplessness. The child believes that it is punished because it is unlovable. At the very least, it develops low self-esteem —at worst, self-loathing and self-destructive behavior. For these children, the world is perceived as a dangerous place, where attention brings the threat of violence, and self-expression becomes an invitation to further pain. Because of extreme fear, many of these children enter into a self-protective dreamlike state, the out-of-body, porous feeling that so many people experience in their daily lives, but which they report to be significantly greater during attacks of anxiety or panic. For adults who have suffered these violations as children, the body remains associated with this trauma, and leaving the body is an unconscious attempt to escape the pain.

Parents or caretakers who use these punishments rationalize their behavior as being for the good of the child. Some cite the Bible as their divine authority and instructor, saying they punish to teach the child the difference between right and wrong, to reinforce good behavior.

What in fact is taught is that it is fine for the powerful to use aggression against the less powerful. (What the child also learns is that authority is violent and untrustworthy.) If the aggression is meted out in the name of love, then love, too, becomes something to be feared or confused with aggression. No wonder, then, that the child, and later the adult, remains terrified of asking for or receiving attention from others, especially those onto whom he or she has projected authority.

Some parents inflict less blatant but equally profound damage on their children because their own early unmet needs make them incapable of responding in a nurturing way to the needs of their offspring.

These are the mothers who adore (rather than love) their children when they are helpless infants but reject the child when it becomes more independent. The child's natural development is experienced by these mothers as disloyalty, for now the child can no longer be used for the mother's gratification. For these children, dependency was rewarded with attention, while self-assertion brought loss of love and therefore fear of abandonment. This lesson, learned and reinforced at so young and vulnerable an age, has conditioned these children to anticipate similar treatment in circumstances that evoke their original experience of injury, so they either hide behind a timid facade or suffer anxiety whenever they are assertive.

Alternatively, a parent with low self-esteem may use the child to try to shore up a fragile sense of self. With such parents, everything that the child does is felt to be a reflection of their value, so the child must be "perfect." Each time the child fails to reach this impossible mark, the parent's ego is further abraded, and in retaliation "love" is withdrawn. The child blames him/herself for this punishment, and "perfection" becomes its goal, with anything less experienced as failure. Thus the child becomes preoccupied with *how* it is doing, rather than *what* it is doing. In other words, its focus, rather than being on inner gratification, becomes exclusively turned outward.

Or, a parent whose life has remained largely unlived may have been forced (or may have chosen) to abandon something that once meant a great deal to him or her. When the child shows talent in this area, the parent may envy the child's ability to pursue and enjoy this treasured, sacrificed activity. In an unconscious desire to spoil the child's attainment, the parent might establish such high standards that they cannot be met. The child, in such a circumstance, assumes that something in itself is lacking and becomes self-conscious and anxious—not only about pursuing this means of self-expression, but in other areas as well.

Many adults who have come to me for help with performance anxiety remember their parents as kind and loving and their childhoods as "normal." When they have looked deeper, however, some have found that even though they were indeed lovingly raised, they did deviate from their true path. They have also learned, to their surprise, that their parents did, in fact, influence their doing so.

They have come to realize that they adopted a way of being chosen to fulfill their parents' own unrealized dreams. Perhaps they became the professional Mom wished she could have been; or they may have been indoctrinated, from childhood, to carry on the family business (or to follow in

Dad's footsteps) despite talents and temperaments that were better suited for something quite different.

Some have learned that because of their parents' attitudes they were (perhaps subtly) led to reject (or be ashamed of) their true masculine or feminine nature.

Some were enlisted to be a companion by a parent in an unhappy marriage, leaving them, paradoxically, both un-parented and inappropriately tied to the parent.

These people have come to see that they denied or distorted their true nature because of confusion, shame, or guilt or, again, because of fear that if they did otherwise, they would not be loved and cared for.

For many, their new insights, rather than destroying their appraisal of their parents as "loving," reinforced this conviction, enabling them to view the past through a wider lens. They were able, for the first time, to see their parents as people who struggled with their own frustrations and disappointments. Their acceptance of the fullness of their parents' humanity became a turning point in their ability to be less demanding of perfection in themselves. It marked the beginning of their freedom from self-sabotage.

The drive toward wholeness is inborn, and we cannot repress our authenticity without consequences. Our unacknowledged genuine impulses and feelings find expression in physical and psychological symptoms—in a feeling of vagueness or of being out of the body, in pains in the chest or the stomach (as when something can't be digested), in backaches (as when something sits too heavily on our shoulders), in headache or blurred vision, in depression—and, for many of us, in anxiety.

Frequently, in one of the psyche's principal means of

making us conscious of our truths, we see our own attitudes in projection. We attribute them to others—as in Marcy's own self-hatred disguised as destructive "Nazi" energy; Olivier's own repressed emotions experienced as the "monster hiding in its dark corner"; our own negative self-judgments attributed to those who are in a position to judge us.

Everything that has ever happened to us remains alive in the psyche—either in consciousness or, though we may have no memory of the occurrences, in the unconscious. Our panic attacks and projections are signals to us that something of great value is struggling for incarnation.

For indeed, what is deeply hidden beneath the fear, still alive and vital, is our true self. It is from this place of truth that the images, memories, and feelings come in our dreams and fantasies. And it is to this place that we turn for help in combating the anxiety that is further depriving us of our aliveness.

Confronting Performance Anxiety:
Steve and Nancy

———————

*We straggle behind our years, hugging our childhood as
if we could not bear to tear ourselves away.*

—C. G. JUNG

NOTHING CAN CHANGE OUR history, for it is part of our fate.
But we can change the ways in which we habitually respond
to situations that evoke old trauma. By confronting the
energy within us that remains as part of the original experience, we can interrupt our automatic fearful reactions so
that new courageous ways of being can now be possible.

Let me show you how the process actually works. We'll
follow the workshop experience of two of the people who
answered my ad in *The New York Times* and subsequently
participated in focus groups.

I'll call them Steve and Nancy.

Steve is an actor, unmarried, with little personal experience in psychological exploration. Nancy is an executive,
married, with a long history of psychoanalytic work. Both
are in their thirties. Through their work on the same exercises, they were led by something within themselves to

markedly different results. And when each repeated an exercise, they were able to go deeper and their work became more significant.

This will be your experience, too, as you do your own work detailed in the next chapter. I do not mean to suggest that your emerging material will be the same as either Nancy's or Steve's. It will not be. Your history is uniquely yours, and the material that your psyche will produce in response to each exercise will also be unique. But Steve's and Nancy's approach to the exercises, their technique, and yours, will be the same.

A word about my participation in the workshop. Please notice that it is Nancy and Steve, not I, who lead the way in their exercises. Rather it would be more accurate to say that we are led into these areas by the psyche of each of them, since neither they nor I had planned the course or outcome of any of their exercises. Their work is directed by something within each of them, called forth in response to their having made the commitment to do this work. You, too, will be led by your inner guide to whatever issues are connected with your fear of being seen and heard.

All the exercises are designed to help us investigate both the symptoms of their performance anxiety and the psychological factors that feed the fear. Since Steve and Nancy were part of a group of four people, each relates to others in the room in early exercises, but later their focus is exclusively inward. We met in a small soundproof rehearsal room for two hours, once a week, for eight weeks. The room was empty except for folding chairs.

Workshop One: Sharpening Focus

I began by asking Nancy and Steve to talk about their stage fright and what they hoped to get out of this workshop.

STEVE: I'm an actor. Suffering from stage fright is probably the worst thing for an actor. Sometimes I don't feel it that much, other times it's crippling.

Sometimes at auditions it gets so bad that I have to walk out of the room. My body gets rigid and my head is either swimming or full of thoughts like Who am I kidding? Am I good enough? Am I wanted?

What I'm hoping to get out of this is the confidence and courage that would enable me to overcome the stage fright, the nervousness, the anxiety. I keep thinking it's confidence because it seems to me that it's when I lose my confidence that I get nervous.

NANCY: I'm Nancy. Like you (to Steve) I need to learn how to speak in public for my career—as soon as I started to speak *now*, my heart started to pound.

I thought the focus group was very helpful because it made me think about things that I hadn't before. It made me realize that perhaps this problem with stage fright isn't just something that happens when I stand up in front of other people. That it affects me in crunch situations on a daily basis with salespeople, my contractor, clients—in any confrontational situation.

I: Confrontational?

NANCY: That's how it feels. But perhaps it's simply that I have trouble asking for what I deserve and insisting on it and not caving—and I have a tendency to cave. And I'm realizing that I do that a lot in a lot of different situations.

I: Okay. Now, Steve, please stand and introduce yourself to each person in the room. And while you're doing that, tell us what's happening in your body and what you're thinking.

STEVE: I feel it a little bit in my body now.

I: What do you feel?

STEVE: It's anticipation. It's a feeling in my chest—a tightening.

I: Allow it to get as big as it wants. Give it real permission.

STEVE: (Takes a minute and breathes deeply) Hi, I'm Steve. And I feel really self-conscious.

I: Can you move in some way that would express what you feel?

STEVE: I guess like this. (Wiggles and flails his arms around) More distance. (Backs out of the circle of our chairs)

I: Does that feel better?

STEVE: Yeah. It feels more clothed or something. But I feel like I'm running away, and I'm tired of doing that.

I: So what would you like to do?

STEVE: Come back. (He does so.) Now I feel like I'm under observation. (Giggles)

I: How does it feel to be under observation?

STEVE: Uncomfortable. I feel possible judgment.

I: What might we be thinking?

STEVE: What's going on with this guy? What's the big deal? Just stand up and say your name.

I: So you're assuming we're judging you?

STEVE: Yeah. I even catch myself doing it in the middle of an audition. I have all this training to put my focus on the other actor, but as soon as I realize that they're watching me, I start to judge myself and I pull myself out of it.

I: So your concentration is shot.

STEVE: Yes, it is. My focus changes from what I'm doing to wondering what they're thinking. And what I feel is the casting director's saying to himself, What a jerk, or that the director is annoyed with me.

I: Well, let's say it's true and you're picking up something from the casting person.

STEVE: Okay.

I: The fact is, it's your time.

STEVE: Right. And I've already invested all the time in getting ready for the audition and going down there, but when I get there I give it up. Just looking for something, almost looking for something to stop me.

I: Yes. Now somewhere you learned to do that. You learned to interfere with just going after what you want.

STEVE: That's right. You're right. I don't allow myself just to go after it.

I: So how can we help you not to give up? If you're just going through the motions, thinking, She wants me to hurry, or, He's not listening to me, then you're not thinking, This is my time.

STEVE: Yeah. I'm not really putting enough of a value on my own time, on what I want do do—

I: Steve, take your time right now and look at each of us. Is that what you see?

STEVE: No. No, I guess not.

I: So whose judgments are these?

STEVE: Mine?

I: Yes, they're yours. Your judgments of yourself, not ours. Please think about this during the week and see if you can catch yourself when you do it.

Steve's first exercise had been born out of an expectation of others' negative judgments, an expectation shared by many people who suffer from performance anxiety.

He had learned to judge himself harshly, to be divided against himself. So our first work with Steve would be to help him to see how he acquired both of these negative expectations.

Now here's Nancy's experience of the same exercise.

NANCY: Hi, I'm Nancy. (She sounds very frightened.) Well, my heart is pounding.

I: That's okay. Just let it pound. Stay with it if you can. Anything that comes up is fine. There's no wrong way to do this.

NANCY: (Almost in tears) It's made me very emotional.

I: That's okay. Don't try to control the emotion. Allow it, and keep going.

NANCY: As I explained to you in the focus group, I had surgery as a young child, and I've had this sensation when I have to get up and give a speech of lying in the hospital bed.

Nancy was so full of feelings that I followed these rather than insisting that she stay with the exercise as outlined. Our feelings are not random—they are the result of our histories. I trusted that Nancy's psyche was taking us where we needed to go to help her to overcome her performance anxiety. And she would have other opportunities to do the exercise as prescribed if these associations proved to be resistance to the process.

> I: Is there anything more you'd like to tell us?
>
> NANCY: Well, it's sort of—there really isn't anybody there. I was about three years old. I was staring across the room at the windows, and either there's no one there at all (her voice breaking a bit), or there is a doctor attending to another child on the other side of the room—or I have this sort of fuzzy image of my father being next to the bed, but not my mother there. (Tears) It's clearly something I have to keep covered up all the time.
>
> I: Yes, I can see that.
>
> NANCY: And I thought it was something that I had done a fair job of covering. How odd to talk about it here.
>
> I: I don't think it's odd at all. I think it means that that experience is in some way connected with your stage fright. Do you feel how much energy you're using to try to control these feelings, Nancy?
>
> NANCY: Yes. Sometimes it's so hard.
>
> I: Go back to the exercise.
>
> NANCY: Hi. My name is Nancy. (Stops, struggling to control her tears)
>
> I: It's all right to let go here.

NANCY: But I don't want to cry. I do that too much anyway. I can't not do it. (Cries)

I: It's okay to cry, but let's see, next time, if you can cry and keep going. If you stay with the work, I'm pretty sure we'll be able to free that energy. We'll come back to this next week.

Through their thoughts, feelings, and memories, Steve and Nancy led us to what would prove to be central elements in their performance anxiety—Steve to his fear of negative judgments and Nancy to her three-year-old self in the hospital. These themes, as you will see, recur for each of them.

Workshop Two: Opening to the Psyche

When we met the following week, I asked for any discoveries as a result of our first session. This is an important part of the work—something you will learn to do as well—for when we are able to observe ourselves more objectively, we can question our old automatic behavior.

Steve jumped in eagerly:

I wanted to tell you that this week, at auditions, I could see that I was wrong. People weren't saying, ''What an idiot, what a jerk, let's get rid of this guy.'' If anything, they were saying nice things. I mean, not even knowing them, having never met them before, it was almost as if you could see in their eyes that they really wanted me to do good.

And Nancy said:

I thought about it a lot. I realized this week how much this fear affects everything I do. How I try to control myself and everyone else with words. And it is a burden, a tremendous strain, a grabber of energy, and I resent that I have to devote so much energy to it. (Tears) This is a deeper problem than I realized before.

Both Steve and Nancy had begun to change their relationship to their anxiety. No longer merely passive victims of their fear, they were now actively engaged in investigating it. By continuing to explore their anxiety, they would change the balance of power in this psychological battle. By supporting their conscious intentions, they were weakening those factors within themselves that sought to defeat their conscious wishes, thereby strengthening their ability to persevere.

I: Okay. Let's go to work again. Steve, do you remember last week's exercise?

STEVE: Hi. I'm Steve. (Tries not to laugh)

I: Allow whatever wants to come up to express itself. (He sniffles, laughs, sniffles.)

STEVE: Hi, I'm Steve. (Again tries not to laugh) Hi, I'm Steve. (Sniffles, laughs, sniffles, laughs)

I: There's something else in there. Let go. Don't control it.

STEVE: (Laughs, then whispers) Hi. I'm Steve.

I: Okay. What can you tell us?

STEVE: I started to notice after you told me to stay with the laughing, there was a little pain underneath the laughing.

I: I'd like you to do the exercise again without controlling anything. If you want to laugh, laugh.

But really laugh. If your body wants to move, allow it.

STEVE: Okay. Hi. I'm Steve. (Shakes his shoulders)

I: What just happened?

STEVE: Felt like I had to shake something off.

I: What was it?

STEVE: A demon? (Laughing) I don't know. It was like some part of me that seems to get in my way.

I: Do that again as fully as you can.

STEVE: (Shakes his body, closes his eyes, and shakes his head as if to say "no") I don't know. I feel like part of me is not cooperating.

I: So you're divided. Pretend that the uncooperative part of you is another person, and put it in that empty chair and talk to it.

STEVE: (Looks at the chair; tentatively) I just wish you'd get out of my way.

I: Does that express what you feel?

STEVE: (Sniffles) It's like a mischievous—

I: Make it real. Try to really see it. Is it he or she?

STEVE: He. He's like a mischievous kid saying, "I'm not getting in the way." Yet in the mischievousness and the way he's saying it, there's something about him knowing—

I: Talk to him.

STEVE: You know you're (laughs) getting in my way. (Softly) I don't want you getting in my way.

I: Do you mean it?

STEVE: (Without conviction) It's time for you to get out of my way.

I: How can you make him listen?

STEVE: You'd better stop laughing at me.

I: Is he laughing at you?

STEVE: He's got a gleam in his eye like ha ha ha ha—

I: Be him.

STEVE: (Hops from foot to foot) Ha ha ha ha ha, like a leprechaun.

I: Be him. Be him talking to you. Don't think about it, just do it.

STEVE: Okay. Um . . . (Laughing) I'm going to fuck you up. (Laughs and sniffles) I'm going to get in your way.

I: What would you do in life if somebody said that to you?

STEVE: (Sniffling) I don't think I'd let them.

I: Well, do something.

STEVE: I think I'm lost—I don't know—

I: Okay. Come sit down.

STEVE: There was also the last thing that popped up was him sort of saying, "You don't deserve it."

I: Okay. What do you think is going on here?

STEVE: Well, I want to do the exercise, but something in me is saying "ha ha ha ha ha" and doesn't want me to. Like at auditions. It's really something in me.

I: Yes. It's something that's a part of you. That's enough for now. Think about this experience from time to time during the week.

As you can see, Steve went farther with the same exercise that he did last week.

Last week his awareness was more intellectual, this week his experience was more deeply felt. Now that he has acknowledged its reality in his psyche, Steve can learn to confront the part of himself that is his obstruction. As yet, this adversarial part still retained the upper hand, but its power would diminish when Steve learned to confront it.

This will be the course of your work, too, as you expose the parts of yourself that are in opposition to your conscious wishes and then learn to confront them.

I had asked each participant to bring in a piece of written material—a speech, an excerpt from a book, a poem—to use as a presentation. This was just another device to bring on performance anxiety so that it could be investigated.

Nancy chose to present a proposal she had made at work. She rushed ahead, her voice rather flat and without enthusiasm. There was no conviction, no authority, in her delivery.

I: Okay. What can you tell us?

NANCY: I'm criticizing myself continuously.

I: Can you "be" the critic and speak for her? What's she saying?

NANCY: (As the critic) There were a couple of subtle points that you didn't make. You seem to know it well enough, but I would expect more of you.

I: More?

NANCY: More means more precision, you need to be unimpeachable, you need to be unable to be contradicted by anybody. You need to be right. You need to be perfect.

I: Perfect?

NANCY: There's probably a two or three percent margin for error there, but that's not a lot. So it has to be approaching perfect.

I: What a slave driver. So she's got a whip.

NANCY: Yeah.

I: What do you want to tell her?

NANCY: (Calmly, flatly) It's not reasonable.

Like Steve, Nancy needed to learn how to confront this part of herself. So I asked questions aimed at helping her deal with her "slave driver."

I: Is that how you want to tell her? If somebody were at you with a whip, what would you say to them?

NANCY: (Flatly) You're beating me up.

I: Is that how you'd say it?

NANCY: (Laughing) No, that's not how I'd say it. I'd be screaming. (Tearfully) I'd probably be crying, frankly. And I've been crying ever since.

I: Ever since what?

NANCY: Ever since I was three years old.

I: What happened when you were three years old?

NANCY: I was being punished for not being perfect.

I: Is that what you thought?

NANCY: Yeah.

I: Who was punishing you?

NANCY: My parents abandoned me in the hospital, the doctors did whatever they had to do to me, and there were people around and they were ignoring me.

I: Who was the most abandoning of the whole lot of them?

NANCY: Well, my parents.

I: Which one?

NANCY: The only one that I visualize is my father. My mother's not there. She should have been there.

I: Okay. Pretend she's sitting in that chair, and talk to her.

NANCY: (Tentatively) Why weren't you there?

I: Really ask her.

NANCY: (Much more forcefully) Why weren't you there? (Laughs)

Nancy's laughter, like Steve's, was a nervous reaction and covered something. But if I focused on it now, she would be led away from where her psyche had directed us—back to the scene in the hospital.

I: Stay with it if you can.

NANCY: (Shouting) Why weren't you there?

I: Tell her how it made you feel.

NANCY: It made me feel abandoned. Abandoned. Like screaming. As depressed as you are all the time.

I: Is there something you would like to do? (Pause) Don't think about it. Just do it.

NANCY: Shake her.

I: Do. Shake her. (She rattles the empty chair.) Do you want to make some noise with that?

NANCY: I can't—I mean, I couldn't scream loud enough.

I: Why not?

NANCY: Well, the place—

I: This is a soundproof room.

Nancy screamed repeatedly.

I: Tell her how it makes you feel.

NANCY: (Heatedly) That's how it makes me feel. It makes me feel like screaming all the time. And all you do is sit there and cry. And after a while you'll admit that (sarcastically) you didn't know, it's not

your fault. It doesn't work. It's not an excuse.
Because basically everything you've done since
then has reinforced that. (Pause; then to me) I feel
calmer now. But I could never say any of that to
her.

I: Whether or not you tell her, you need to say it for
your little girl who couldn't say it for herself. We'll
stop here now, Nancy, and give you a chance to
digest and think about all of this.

Nancy, as a defense, is overly intellectual. (She has taught
herself to be this way in an attempt to deal with her pain, her
feelings of abandonment.) It was necessary to get below this
habitual means of self-protection so that the real Nancy
could emerge. And we were just beginning to do so.

Her psyche had led us back to her three-year-old self in
the hospital. She was learning to speak for, and relate to, the
child who was still very much alive in her. By giving
the child her voice, she is beginning to lessen the energy in
the child's pain so that she can move on.

As you can see, this long-ago hospital experience, and her
feelings about it, became more specific. We stopped now
because we did not want to flood Nancy with too much
material all at once. She needed time, as you will, to integrate her experiences in these exercises.

Our childhoods remain alive in us, and our energy is
caught in unexplored childhood trauma. We cannot erase
the trauma, but we can change our relationship to it. We can
diminish the impact it has on our lives by exploring and
facing what we felt when we were traumatized.

Workshop Three: Contacting the Inner Child

We began again with our first exercise—that of each member of the workshop introducing him/herself.

> STEVE: (Trying unsuccessfully to suppress a laugh) Hi. I'm Steve.
>
> I: Stay with it. Let it take you anywhere it wants to.
>
> STEVE: (Laughs a bit and clears his throat) Hi. I'm Steve.
>
> I: What's in all of that? Give it words. I feel what?
>
> STEVE: Uh (pause) I guess silly.
>
> I: Okay. And how does it feel to feel silly?
>
> STEVE: I don't know.
>
> I: Sure you do.
>
> STEVE: Awkward, I guess—
>
> I: Okay. What does "awkward" feel like? Can you let your body express that?

Steve wiggled.

> I: Yes. Let it out. Exaggerate it.
>
> STEVE: Now something like this. I'm not sure. (Goes into a fetal position)
>
> I: Okay. What's going on now?
>
> STEVE: I'm hiding.
>
> I: Hiding. Do it more. Go all the way with it.

He covered his head with his hands, still in a fetal position. This posture was a total surprise to me—there was no way of knowing that "silly" and "awkward" would lead us here.

> I: Now from the place, as that hiding person, introduce yourself.
>
> STEVE: (Still in the fetal position, head covered) Hi, I'm Steve.

I: And tell us what you're experiencing.

STEVE: I'm just feeling like a little kid.

I: Great.

STEVE: Like myself as a little kid.

I: How old are you?

STEVE: (Laughs) I'm thinking about second grade. I'm seven.

I: You're seven in second grade. What are you thinking about?

STEVE: It was the first day of school, a new school. And for some reason I hid under the desk—

I: Why? Be back there. Be that little kid.

STEVE: I think I was doing it for attention.

I: For attention? From whom?

STEVE: From classmates, from the teacher for acceptance—

I: Acceptance?

STEVE: Or I don't know—was I just hiding 'cause I felt uncomfortable and I (pause) I'm not sure.

I: Can you put the teacher in your fantasy? What's she saying?

STEVE: (Sternly, quietly) She's saying, "Get out from underneath that desk."

I: And what do you want to say to her?

STEVE: What I want to say to her is "Fuck off."

I: Tell her to fuck off, then.

STEVE: Fuck off. (Louder) Fuck off.

I: Tell her why you're doing it.

STEVE: (Long pause; then, as if to himself) I need love and attention.

I: What does she say?

STEVE: She's confused by this.

I: Tell her again.

STEVE: I need love and attention. (Sniffles and sighs deeply) I need love and attention.

I: What's going on?

STEVE: It feels good.

I: Yes, it feels good to tell the truth.

STEVE: But it's scary. I think I would have avoided it if I hadn't had this goal.

I: What goal?

STEVE: To overcome this, you know, this anxiety and the fear.

I: Why would you have avoided it, Steve?

STEVE: 'Cause it was uncomfortable.

I: What's uncomfortable about it?

STEVE: Admitting that I need love and attention. That I'm thirty years old and I still have the needs of a seven-year-old child.

I: How about reframing it and saying that that seven-year-old child in you still needs love and attention. It's a little more friendly that way, isn't it?

STEVE: Yes, I guess so.

I: And why would you not want love and attention as a thirty-year-old or a fifty- or a seventy-year-old? It's human.

STEVE: Right.

I: Where did you get the idea that you weren't supposed to have those needs?

STEVE: I guess, you know, my upbringing.

I: Ah. Well, we'll get there soon.

Steve's work took him back to being seven years old. Was this a memory of something that had happened in reality when he was seven? I had no idea. But whether or not it happened in the outside world, it was alive in the inner one. And it was the inner world that we were dealing with here.

Later in the session I asked Steve to present some written material to the group. Again, as in the introduction exercise, he was to tune in to his body and his thoughts and to follow whatever impulses he might have.

> STEVE: I'm stopping myself before I even begin.
>
> I: What's interfering with your starting?
>
> STEVE: This is a monologue that I have a particular problem with. Part of me feels like I should have prepared it as an audition in order to bring it in here.
>
> I: Should?
>
> STEVE: Right.
>
> I: "Shoulds" are always imposed on us. What do *you* want? You chose that because *you* wanted to do it.
>
> STEVE: Right. Originally I thought I would just read it, now I'm feeling like it should have been prepared—
>
> I: All right. Be the part of you that tells you you "should" have done it differently, and let him tell you how you're doing it wrong.
>
> STEVE: (With annoyance) If you were going to get the most out of this exercise, you would have brought in this monologue prepared as if this were an audition situation. And instead you just brought in a piece of paper and you're going to read it. You're not going to get anything out of that. You're wasting everyone's time.

I: What do you want to say to him?

STEVE: I feel in agreement with him.

I: So here's your critical part again.

STEVE: Yeah.

I: Now where did that come from? Who criticized you as a kid? Don't think about it. Just answer. Who criticized you?

My question was based on my knowledge that we are not born self-critical but *learn* to be that way. And usually our excessive self-criticism reflects the treatment we received as children.

STEVE: I think everybody criticized me as a kid.

I: Who?

STEVE: You know, my parents and my older brother, and they were very strict at school.

I: Who comes to mind first?

STEVE: (Defeatedly) My dad.

I: Let him talk to you. Let him tell you how you failed again tonight. (Pause) Just do it. Don't think about it.

STEVE: (With conviction) Jesus Christ, Steve, if you really wanted to do this, you would have done it right. You're wasting your time. You're—you just—you're not going to amount to anything. It's not gonna happen for you. It didn't happen for me, so what makes you think that it's going to work for you? You're such a pain in the ass. (Stops)

I: Don't think. Just answer him.

STEVE: (Tentatively) That hurts.

I: Is that how you want to say it?

STEVE: (Very tentatively) You've got to get off my back now.

I: I wouldn't listen to you if you talked that way to me. Do you mean it?

STEVE: (Loudly) You've gotta get off my back now—'cause I gotta go on with my own life.

I: Yes. Keep going.

STEVE: It's over. This segment is over and now is where I pick up with my life and I move on. And if that means leaving you behind, then that's what I'm going to have to do. (Long pause)

I: What's going on now?

STEVE: I feel sad.

I: Then let the sad feelings out. Tell him how you feel.

STEVE: Well, I'm in pain once again, and at this moment you're (laughs) responsible for it.

I: What do you feel?

STEVE: (Deeply felt) I feel lost.

I: Tell him.

STEVE: I just feel lost. I feel there's really nothing I can do about it sometimes.

I: Right now how do you feel?

STEVE: (Laughing) I feel like kicking him, but there's like—

I: Okay. You feel like kicking him and what you're doing is laughing.

STEVE: Yeah.

I: You're sabotaging what you're feeling. Kick him. (He laughs.) Go ahead, kick him. Don't think about it. Just do it. Kick him. (He kicks the chair.)

STEVE: And then I feel bad.

I: Then feel bad. Then tell him you feel bad. Stay with your feelings and keep the dialogue going.

STEVE: I'm sor— (Laughs and stops)

I: Keep laughing if you want to laugh, but keep going.

STEVE: You're not (laughing) even here for me to get angry with (laughs)—

I: Keep laughing if you want to laugh, but keep going.

STEVE: (Without conviction) I want to be able to make something of my life, and I don't want to be held back by all your judgments. I want to go straight ahead.

I: Tell him.

STEVE: I want to go straight ahead.

I: Tell him again.

STEVE: I'm going to go straight ahead and you're not going to stop me.

I: Tell him again.

STEVE: I'm sorry, Dad, but I'm going to go straight ahead and you're not going to stop me.

I: What are you sorry about?

STEVE: I feel like somehow I'm hurting his feelings.

I: Ah. You said, "It didn't happen for me, so what makes you think it's going to happen for you?" What do you suppose that meant?

STEVE: I don't know. (Thinks for a moment) He didn't want me to succeed?

I: I think that's right. It sounds like he didn't want you to succeed, and you must have sensed that. You're going to have to say good-bye to your father if you want to move on.

STEVE: I do.

I: Okay. Then that's where your work will lead us. We'll stop here for today.

Just as we are taken from one feeling to the next in life, so these exercises take us from one feeling to the next. And if we are really allowing ourselves to be directed by something within, we cannot predict what these feelings will be, but whatever they are, we must follow them.

We say we want to change, but change means leaving the old familiar patterns that began in childhood. We adopted these ways of being because they seemed to offer us protection against pain, against abandonment. No matter how painful they may be, no matter how much we may say (and believe) that we want to change, there is in reality a tremendous pull to stay with what is familiar.

By making conscious his father's negative impact, Steve had the opportunity to confront his own ambivalence about leaving him and getting on with his own life.

This time, in our third workshop, he was able to take a stand.

For Nancy's exercise, I decided simply to follow her psyche and go directly to her experience in the hospital.

I: Sit in the chair, please, as comfortably as you can.

Then, slowly, I took Nancy through a relaxation exercise. This was designed to quiet her consciousness and allow her inner self to emerge more fully. I used Nancy's words from earlier exercises so as to follow rather than lead her.

I: You're a little girl. You're three years old. And you're in the hospital. You're in that bed. Your mother is not there. You dimly perceive other children in other beds. Just be there in the bed.

Nancy fought her tears. She has allowed herself to be transported back in time.

I: It's okay. It's okay. (She is crying now.) What do you want to say?

NANCY: (Crying and with force) It's so not okay. (With rage) It's so not okay.

I: What's not okay?

NANCY: (Crying, with anger) To be here.

I: Tell me about it.

NANCY: (Crying) It's dark. I'm alone. I don't know what I'm doing here. In some ways I can't remember ever being anywhere else but here. It just goes on and on and on and on. And sometimes it's daylight and sometimes it's dark and it's always here.

I: What do you want to do?

NANCY: (Crying into her hands) I want to go home.

I: Why are you staying?

NANCY: (Wailing like a three-year-old child) I can't move.

I: Why not?

NANCY: (Crying, loudly) I have a cast from my hip to my ankle to my foot. I can't walk, I can't do anything. I'm completely crushed. I'm completely helpless. I'm totally trapped. I don't know what I did to deserve this. All I can do is scream.

I: Scream.

NANCY: (Cries, screams, sobs) All I can do is scream. There's a window next to my bed, in the hallway. And the nurse is making faces at me like "Shut up. You're waking everyone up. Shut up. You can go on screaming all you want, nothing's ever going to

happen to you. You're always going to be here.''
Matter of fact, I always have been.

I waited for a few moments to allow her time to calm herself.

I: Now you're you, and the three-year-old is here, too. She's right in front of you. Talk to her.

NANCY: I know how you feel. (Crying) I really do know how you feel.

I: What else would you like to say to her?

NANCY: (Continues to cry) Part of me wants to go back inside you and play it differently. Maybe by being back inside of you, at thirty-six, we could make the outcome different.

I: Well, you can be back inside her. You can do anything in your imagination that you want. What would be different? (Nancy cries.)

NANCY: Maybe I would just scream more. Although I think I gotta do something else but scream. My parents told me that they came to see me twice a day. Actually I have no recollection of that. They would always bring me a little toy every time they visited, and at the time of the visit they would wait till I was distracted with the new toy, and when I wasn't watching, they'd leave.

I: Tell them how it made you feel.

NANCY: (Crying) Oh, horrible. It was horrible. I have no recollection of that, but the idea of that is so awful. It is. How could somebody do that? And I'd look up and they'd be gone. And they'd come again the same night and they would do the same thing. They'd be gone. They would just disappear. As if I weren't supposed to notice. They just wouldn't be there anymore. So I just screamed the whole time I was there. How much more could I have screamed? It wasn't going to do any good. It didn't do any good. I'm still screaming.

I: Tell the child that now that you're talking with her you will keep that contact going, that you're not going to leave her.

NANCY: I won't leave you. I can't leave you.

I: Tell her that you're going to be there for her from now on.

NANCY: (Softly) I'll be there for you from now on.

I: And that you'll help her.

NANCY: I'll help you as much as I can.

I: Does she hear you?

NANCY: Yes.

I: Does she believe you?

NANCY: Yeah. She knows I'm trying.

I: Now, Nancy, allow yourself to be back in this room, and when you're ready slowly open your eyes.

The room was silent. I waited for a few minutes before going on.

I: I'd like to give you some homework.

NANCY: Fine.

I: Do you get upset during the week—do your feelings get hurt?

NANCY: Sometimes.

I: Okay. If that happens, can you sit quietly and take your three-year-old self into your lap and just hold her, and if she wants to scream, let her scream? Can you do that?

NANCY: I'll try.

What did we learn?

Nancy's three-year-old self was still suffering and kept the adult Nancy stuck in that old pain. By going back to the child and giving the child her voice, Nancy would begin to change her relationship to her trauma and be able to move on.

Workshop Four: Evoking the Past

I brought a new exercise to the workshop.

> I: I would like each of you to stand, one at a time, and say your name repeatedly. Allow yourself to do anything that you feel moved to do, but don't stop repeating your name. Keep doing this until something else within you forces itself into the exercise. Steve, let's start with you.
>
> STEVE: (Softly) Steve Steve Steve. (Begins to laugh)
>
> I: Stay with that.
>
> STEVE: Steve Steve Steve Steve Steve.
>
> I: Louder
>
> STEVE: Steve. Steve. Steve.
>
> I: Louder.
>
> STEVE: Steve. Steve. Steve.
>
> I: Louder.
>
> STEVE: Steve Steve Steve Steve Steve (Laughs and shouts his name and laughs) Steve Steve Steve.
>
> I: Louder.
>
> STEVE: Steve Steve Steve. (Sounds as if he is calling someone else whose name is Steve) Steve. I find I don't like saying my name.
>
> I: Why not?
>
> STEVE: It just sounds weird.

I: What does it sound like?

STEVE: It sounds like—something about it, about my own voice, reminded me of the tone of my father's voice when he got annoyed. Steve. With that little punch at the end of it.

I: And how did that feel?

STEVE: I didn't really want to be reminded of pissing my father off, of letting him down.

I: Is that what that tone would have implied?

STEVE: Yeah.

I: That he was pissed off, that you let him down?

STEVE: Yeah.

I: Put your father in the chair and ask him why he is pissed off.

STEVE: What's the problem, Dad?

I: And what does he say? Play both parts.

STEVE: What's the problem, Dad? "Nothing. Nothing's the problem." That's total denial and I want to know what the problem is.

I: Well, you said it before. You said you let him down. What were the words?

STEVE: He could never—"I could never trust you, Steve. I could never trust you." Well, you never really gave me a chance.

I: How did you feel when he never gave you a chance?

STEVE: I feel cheated. (Voice is ringing) I feel cheated. I was cheated. You cheated me, and there's no way I can make it up now. I feel like you didn't want to have me. And I feel—actually I feel like that's a fact. So I'm here and you should have done what you could have instead of totally just brushing me off.

I: Is that what he did? He brushed you off?

STEVE: Brushed me off. Pushed me out of the way. (Voice rising) Patted me on the fucking head. That was the attention that I got, that was the whole bulk of it—being patted on the head like a dog. (Quietly) I'm not a dog. I'm your son. You can't turn your back on me anymore. Say something. "I'm sorry." He's saying, "I'm sorry." And, "How was I supposed to know?" He had no idea what was going on in my head. (Louder) But you were the adult and I was the kid. And if you had just opened your eyes and looked, you would have seen. Dad, I needed you. I needed a father. (Louder) I needed a father. You disgust me. (To me) Now I feel sorry for him.

I: Do you? (Pause)

STEVE: No, I'm feeling sorry for myself, and I also feel like—useless.

I: Tell him.

STEVE: Useless. I always felt like an outsider. I felt like I didn't belong. And it hurt. It made me feel like a freak. Like a misfit. I'm not.

I: Tell him again.

STEVE: I'm not a misfit. I'm not a misfit. I'm not a misfit.

I: (After a few moments) Let's end here.

Later in the session, as Steve laughed repeatedly while presenting some written material, I stopped him.

I: I'm going to stop you because the laughing covers something. And it happens during every exercise.

STEVE: Right.

I: If you really let it go, it would lead us to whatever it's covering. Your father is rejecting you, and you're laughing. What do you make of that?

STEVE: Seems like if I laughed, it was in order to get him off my back or to try to make him laugh about it.

I: Well, what we need to do is to get to the feelings underneath the laughter. So if you want to laugh, that's fine, but let it go all the way. Okay? Now your father is saying you didn't do it right. What's he saying? What are the words? Be him. (Long pause)

STEVE: "If you were serious about this, you would have chosen the right thing." (Sighs) I just want to tell him to get off my back.

I: Tell him.

STEVE: (Softly) Get off my back.

I: Tell him so he hears you.

STEVE: (Louder) Get off my back. (Louder still) Get off my back. It's just something to read. It doesn't have to be anything. It can be anything. Get off my fucking back. I can use this. This is all right. This is not a big deal. Just forget about it. You don't know what you're talking about.

I: Now. From that place, without changing anything, start reading.

He read his material. His delivery was forceful, and he did not laugh.

I: What's the difference? What have you learned?

STEVE: What a big deal my father still is in my life. And that when I laugh—I've always told myself it's because I'm uncomfortable—but is it always to cover my anger? I just had no idea I was so angry.

Again Steve was asking himself good questions. He was using the work well.

Now it was Nancy's turn.

NANCY: Nancy Nancy Nancy Nancy Nancy Nancy. It doesn't feel like anything.

I: Say it louder.

NANCY: Nancy Nancy Nancy Nancy Nancy. I'm back in the hospital. Nancy Nancy Nancy Nancy. It's where I started out in the first place. My mother is standing at the end of the bed. Nancy Nancy Nancy Nancy. (Begins to cry)

I: Stay with it. Just keep going.

NANCY: Nancy Nancy Nancy Nancy Nancy calm down, Nancy.

I: Who's saying calm down?

NANCY: My mother.

I: What do you want to say? Answer her.

NANCY: I can't calm down. (Tears) "Calm down. Be quiet. Be nice."

I: What do you want to tell her?

NANCY: I can't be nice. I'm scared. (Tears) I've spent my whole life being nice. Everything you taught me was about being nice. Before then and since then everything's about being nice. I don't always feel like being nice.

I: Go back to your name.

NANCY: Nancy Nancy Nancy. You know, all the things I've just said I've known for years.

I: You have to tell her. How do you feel about her?

NANCY: (Tears) Betrayed. I feel really betrayed. I feel like you did a really lousy job. You really screwed up. You have not the faintest idea in how many ways you've screwed up. And I can't confront you about it because all you'll do is cry and say—

I: You are confronting her.

NANCY: —you didn't know.

I: You are confronting her. And she's saying, "I didn't know"?

NANCY: That's what she's saying.

I: Okay. Be her now. And then be yourself. Play both parts.

NANCY: "I didn't know." But you should have known. You should have been able to figure it out. You're a coward. You've lived behind your cowardice for years. Now she's crying.

I: Keep going.

NANCY: (Tears) I have tremendous contempt for you because you won't deal with anything. You won't deal with me in any real way. You don't do anything but cry. You just make excuses.

I: What's her excuse?

NANCY: "I didn't know. (Tears) Don't say that. I did my best. I tried."

I: Tell her how that makes you feel. Full out. Full out. Don't think about it.

NANCY: (Shouting) It's dishonest. You've walked around your whole life feeling sorry for yourself, making excuses for yourself, you want me to buy into the excuses, I bought into the excuses, I made excuses for you for a very long time. There are sacred areas in you life that I'm not supposed to confront.

I: Why not?

NANCY: Lack of charity on my part.

I: Be uncharitable.

NANCY: (Calmly) You've always felt like a loser. You've always felt like you've lost out on a lot of things. My father was your savior. All you cared about was him. It made me feel really horrible.

I: So it's not just the hospital.

NANCY: Oh no. The hospital was just the icing on the cake. Long before I realized there was a problem in the hospital, I realized there was a problem with them.

I: How do you feel about her?

NANCY: I resent her a lot. And the older I get the harder time I have being with her. I just feel she's really pathetic.

I: She may be really pathetic, but look how power-fully she still affects you. It will help you finally to come to terms with her if you release your feelings and actively engage with her in your imagination.

Workshop Five: Confronting the Critic

The work did not end with the session but resonated throughout the week.

NANCY: I used the technique you taught me last week, and it worked—your idea of holding the three-year-old on my lap and telling her I'm with her. I was having the latest in the repeating series of arguments with my husband (laughs) and I got really upset and I thought of your idea of speaking for her. I didn't even think about it that long, but it was the combination of thinking about it and hearing my mother say to "be nice." And it gave me tremendous resolve and a sort of clarity about what I felt that I just wouldn't ordinarily have had.

I: That's terrific.

NANCY: Yeah, and I was really crying while I was thinking about this, but then after a while it stopped. And I stood up, and I just told him what I thought, and he took it. And I was able to go on and do what I needed to do. And it just made me much more forceful than I would have been otherwise, and much less ambivalent about what I needed to do.

I: Why do you suppose it worked?

NANCY: Because I was honoring my feelings. Yeah. I was standing with myself.

STEVE: I also had something to tell you. I got a job, and this particular commercial was a direct result of the work that we've done here. Because it became one of those things about looking into the camera and being forceful. And when I was working on the copy, I figured if my father comes up, I'll go into the exercise. But he didn't come up. And I realized it's not so much about pinning it on my father and leaving it there—and the guilt that I felt with that—as much as it is that it's time to confront him. Time to confront him and move on. And that doesn't mean that I have to love him less or that I can't forgive him. It just means that the feelings have to be voiced.

NANCY: But I'm not sure I can really say these things to my mother.

STEVE: Does she need to confront her mother in person?

I: No. It can be done in her imagination. That's the point of these exercises. That's what makes them so valuable.

STEVE: (Jumping in) I have no choice in the matter. My dad is dead.

I: (I am stunned.) I didn't know your father was dead. Maybe you told us—

NANCY: No, he didn't.

I: But I thought your father was alive from the way you've been behaving about him.

STEVE: Whoa. (Laughs)

NANCY: Yeah. I had no idea.

STEVE: I never, I never . . . ?

NANCY: No, you never mentioned it.

STEVE: Yes, five years ago.

I: Now you see how alive your father is for you? We both felt that he was still alive. And what force he continues to exert in your psyche. But you know, it's like when I say to Nancy, "Take your three-year-old on your lap." How is she going to do that except in her imagination?

Steve's father had seemed alive for us because he was so alive in Steve's psyche. Soon, you will see how this energy of "father" will undergo a transformation as the result of Steve's work.

Later in the session Steve read a piece of material.

I: Anything you can tell us about that?

STEVE: Lots of judgment.

I: Now start it again, and put the critical part of you in the chair. Every time he intrudes on your concentration, verbalize what he is saying to you.

STEVE: Okay.

I: Don't worry about finishing the text. Just allow him to come forward.

Steve began reading again, then interrupted himself.

STEVE: He's saying (loudly), "You're stupid for doing it this way—"

I: Be him.

STEVE: You're stupid for doing it this way. (Pause)

I: What else is he saying? Keep going. (He laughs.) Don't let the laughter stop you.

STEVE: He's driving me crazy. "You're a waste of time, you're not ever going to be able to do this."

I: Get into a dialogue with him.

STEVE: Why are you preventing me from doing this?

I: What does he say?

STEVE: That I'm not worth it.

I: Let's hear him say that to you.

STEVE: (Dispiritedly) You're not worth it. You're not worth all the trouble and the time. (Pause)

I: (I open a large paper bag and hand him a padded bat.) Okay. This is called an encounter bat. (He laughs.) Now, this is a wonderful toy. It's got a handle in the middle. You take it with two hands and you can whack with it. You can use it if you want to, you don't have to if you don't want to. (I put it near him.)

STEVE: Okay. (Picks up the bat)

I: Now let him talk to you.

STEVE: (Delightedly) He's scared now. (Laughs fully)

I: What's he scared of?

STEVE: (Still laughing) The bat. I'm going to smash you to smithereens with this bat. He's kinda quiet. (Laughs)

I: How does it feel to have a bat?

STEVE: Empowering.

I: Okay. So you have a weapon—

STEVE: (Shakes it back and forth happily) I think I'll hold on to it just in case. (Laughing) He doesn't want to say a word.

I: Yes. He's scared of you now.

STEVE: Yeah.

I: You've got something to use on him now.

STEVE: Yeah.

I: What is that?

STEVE: (Pause) It's my anger. I've got my anger.

I: Yes. When you don't back down, something changes. So you give him his power by backing down.

STEVE: (To the chair) You're a sneaky son of a bitch. I feel like you've sabotaged me an awful lot in my life, and I'm not gonna let you do it anymore. I'm not gonna let you sabotage my life anymore. And I'm not gonna laugh when you laugh just because it eases your pain, your discomfort. And I'm not gonna laugh just to make you feel more comfortable. And I'm not gonna give up my feelings.

I: You have to be heard.

STEVE: Right.

I: You have to go for broke.

STEVE: Yes. I know I do.

In many families the child gets the message that his or her fear is allowed, even encouraged, while his or her anger is forbidden. Earlier we helped Steve to acknowledge his anger, but he continued to tiptoe around it, laughing rather than expressing his real feelings. During this exercise, he was able to reaffirm that the laughing covered his anger and, further, that his anger helped him overcome his inner adversarial voice. He was learning that his anger displaced his fear.

Workshop Six: Dealing with the Difficult Child

Steve did not participate in this session because he was working again.

Nancy began the naming exercise, but her concentration seemed to be on a business problem.

> NANCY: I'm not by any means incompetent, but I walk around with this kind of nagging fear that I'm going to forget something major.
>
> I: Who's scared?
>
> NANCY: (Becoming tearful) I guess the three-year-old.
>
> I: Can you take her on your lap? What does she want to say to you? (Long pause)
>
> NANCY: She feels not very confident. She feels completely unable to strategize. She feels completely helpless. I think there's always been complaints that I'm not doing well enough.
>
> I: From whom?

NANCY: (Sounding a bit resentful) From her.

I: Well, talk with her. She's complaining that you're not doing well enough? She sounds like a bit of a brat to me.

NANCY: (Laughing) Yeah.

I: What would you like to say to her?

NANCY: (Crying) I'm doing the best that I can. (Sniffling) I'm doing damn well, thank you. I exceeded everybody's expectations by a long shot.

I: Well, you know, this is a real little girl. This is not an idealized little girl.

NANCY: Right.

I: Have you ever seen a three-year-old? Sometimes they're a real pain in the ass. (Nancy laughs.) So let's not idealize this little girl. Let's let her be real.

NANCY: (With strength) Right.

I: You have to deal with her in whatever way she comes up. If she's having a tantrum, you may or may not want to give in to that, like with a real kid. It's not good always to indulge a child. And it doesn't surprise me that your child may be a brat considering how many times she was told to be "nice." Whenever we live too one-sidedly, the other side remains in the unconscious and grows in power. Finally it has to make itself known in some way.

Nancy had worked with her inner child several times now, and each time the result had been a different one. Now, as the child became more like a real child, another facet of her personality emerged. This moved us closer to the truth of Nancy's relationship with herself.

I: During the week, see how much work you can do on your own.

If you find you're getting very frightened—you may not be able to do it in the moment, but as soon as you can—look for two things.

One is, what just happened? Right before you felt frightened, what happened? Is there something that you wanted to say that you didn't say? Was there an impulse you had that you didn't follow through on? So that you abandoned yourself?

For example, Steve called because he couldn't be here tonight. He said that while he was shooting a commercial last week—it was going great—suddenly he realized that he was getting very nervous. And in our tracing it, for just a few minutes on the phone, he realized that he had worked for six hours straight and was tired, but he was afraid to ask for a break. Afraid they would think he was a pain in the ass. So he denied what he needed. And because he denied the impulse, and didn't value what he needed for himself, his stage fright took over.

Our childhoods will always remain alive in us. And our energy is caught in the places of trauma that haven't been worked through. Assume then that the wounded child is alive in you and holding energy that you need for your life. And the child needs your acceptance, your strength, love, intelligence, and even your boundaries, to support it and help it to heal its wounds.

Workshop Seven: Getting to the Heart of the Matter

Again there was excited feedback about the week's discoveries.

> STEVE: I did another commercial that was a really hard one. And at one point I did get into the criticism. It was for a magazine, and I had the magazine and was holding it—and on the breaks when that negativity really came up, the criticism, I hit my father over and over with the magazine. (Laughs loudly) I would say to myself (laughs), Stop stop (laughs loudly and happily) stop, and it gave me control. And it also reignited my sense of humor.

> I: Great. Okay. Any questions? You look—

> STEVE: Well, I'm pretty amazed. You know?

> I: Amazed that the work works?

> STEVE: Yeah. I guess I didn't quite believe it.

He read again from a presentation, rushing ahead, making a few misstatements.

> I: Who in you becomes impatient with your work? What part of you? The part of you that's impatient, put it in the chair.

> STEVE: Okay.

> I: And what's that part saying?

> STEVE: (With contempt) ''Aw, come on, get it right. Jesus Christ.'' Sort of a whining, a lot of whining—

> I: Well, talk to it.

> STEVE: Give me a break. ''Oh, why can't you just get it right?'' 'Cause I'm a human being. (Tentatively) And I'd like to see you do a better job.

I: Yes. Now, with that attitude, pick up the copy and start to read it.

Steve read the copy more slowly and without flaws.

I: What was different that time?

STEVE: At one point I felt myself rushing and I said, I'm not gonna rush. I guess the difference is giving myself permission to take the time and to do it my way.

I: Yes. You stood up for yourself.

We returned to Nancy's work. She plunged right in.

NANCY: With every presentation I do there's this text editor. The words have to be perfect at all times—

I: Put that part of you in the chair.

NANCY: My mother commenting on it.

I: Nancy, this is not Mom now, this is a part of you that's demanding perfection. Talk with that part of yourself.

NANCY: Being in pain and being hospitalized is not because you were being punished. It's just what happened. (Crying) The fact that it happened at all is completely random. You gotta let it go.

I: Now what's she saying?

NANCY: I'm looking at the hospital ward.

I: Okay—

NANCY: (Loudly) It doesn't matter whether it was random. I'm entitled to be angry about this. Even now. Because it was so awful. And I don't want to let you stop suffering in this whole thing.

I: Why not?

NANCY: I guess there's some self-justification in continuing to suffer.

I: What's the self-justification?

NANCY: I don't know.

I: Tell her that you want her to suffer.

NANCY: I want you to suffer. (Sobbing and shouting)
I want you to suffer. It feels so ridiculous to be
saying this. It's like—it's going away when I say it,
which is good, but (pause) I don't know. I'm
getting confused.

I: Stay with what you're feeling. If you get intellectual, you're pulling yourself out of your feelings.
Now what does she say?

NANCY: She says, "I'm gonna keep coming after
you."

I: Ask her why.

NANCY: Why? " 'Cause I have nothing else to do.
Part of my reason for being would cease to exist if
I didn't." Well, why do you have to exist? " 'Cause
I'm a part of you." (Pause) Maybe this is the way
I keep going. What would life be like without it? I
have no idea. (Pause) I don't know. It's very
depressing. I can't go any further.

I: That's okay. You've done good work. But let's look
at it. In your dialogue, it sounded as though your
identity is intertwined with this negative destructive naysaying supercritical aspect of you.

NANCY: Yeah, I noticed that, too.

I: Can you imagine what life would be like without
it?

NANCY: No. (Long pause) Absolutely not.

Again and again we returned to this scene as we went deeper and deeper into the workings of Nancy's psyche. This startling discovery of Nancy's own commitment to her suffering would now have to be integrated.

Workshop Eight: The Work Reaffirmed

Again Steve was eager to share his discoveries during the week.

> STEVE: Something happened to me at church on Sunday. I was in a different church, and there's this ritual where they say "Peace be with you" and you say hello to people around you. And I reached over and said hello to someone, and then I turned around and there was an older man who looked like my dad. We shook hands, and as I looked in his eyes, this joy was in his eyes, and he said things like "How nice it is to meet you" and just lots of wonderful things. And after that, I came back home and I thought what a wonderful thing it would have been to have had that growing up, you know? And running to Dad, and Dad, you know, being excited. I mean, the complete opposite of the way he was. And I know that would have made a big difference in my life. Because when I see acceptance in other people's eyes I know it, but I never felt that as a kid. I could never have labeled it till now, you know?

When we work on the psyche, as you will see, mysterious things happen in our life. This is because our work has

CONFRONTING PERFORMANCE ANXIETY

opened psychic connections to the world and to each other that contradict our ideas of cause and effect.

Steve's "chance meeting" at church was an example of what Jung called "synchronicity"—where meaningful coincidences occur with no apparent cause. It is as if the outer event is "arranged" to reaffirm the changes that are happening in the inner world.

Once Steve was able to stand up to his rejecting father, the impact of his father's negativity was no longer so powerful. There was now the possibility of having positive experiences with people who evoked "father"—directors and other people in authority. And the inner authoritative voice, the energy taken in from his father, could now be forgiving and supportive.

These so-called synchronistic happenings are thrilling and available to anyone who is open to them. They have a numinous quality, making them feel intended as a message of confirmation by something outside of everyday reality.

Through this work, Steve learned that he diminished himself so that he would stay connected with his father. Now he must practice being his full size.

I asked that he present something with which he had a lot of trouble—something embarrassing, something that would demand exposure. I wanted him to dare to go for broke, to be as big as possible.

He gathered himself before he started, taking his time. He spoke with authority. It was a piece he had written about his father. It was very moving, and we were silent for a moment when he finished.

STEVE: That's the end.

I: It was very free and brave.

103

NANCY: It was terrific.

STEVE: I wrote it a few years ago.

NANCY: That was so good.

STEVE: Really?

NANCY: Yeah. I couldn't tell at first if it was a piece of dialogue or a monologue in a play. But at the end it seemed to me that you wrote it. I just thought the script was wonderful, the delivery was wonderful. It was like you were there.

I: Yes.

Steve laughed.

I: It was so you.

NANCY: It was you, but I could also see you on a stage doing it. And it was just utterly convincing. I was so moved.

I: What was your experience? What was the difference in presenting this work?

STEVE: I just took it real slow and honest because I wanted to make sure that I allowed my feelings to come through. 'Cause, of course, that's what I'm working on, what I'm here for. (Laughs) And what was interesting was that I was also surprised in a couple of places by what came up. I didn't make anything happen, and I didn't watch myself. I just wanted it to be whatever it was.

Nancy also gave a final presentation.

I: Now, did you notice that we were sitting on the edge of our seats?

NANCY: Right.

I: Right? I don't think you saw it.

NANCY: I think I saw it, I tuned it out.

I: Now, really see it. How does it feel that we're leaning forward listening to you?

NANCY: (Laughs) It's making me nervous. Like, oh shit. Now I'm going to have to really remember how perfect it was.

I: Okay. The part of you that wants you to suffer—have that part of you talk to you.

NANCY: You spend so much time preparing, you worry about what the other person is thinking, you assume they're analyzing you with the same microscopic intensity that you're analyzing them. That won't do any good. You can never get away from me.

I: Now be her and let her tell you how you can never get away from her.

NANCY: It's hopeless.

I: Why is it hopeless?

NANCY: Because I'm always gonna be there.

I: Why?

NANCY: Because I've been following you around for as long as you can remember.

I: Why is that? Why won't you let Nancy off the hook? (Pause) Go for it, Nancy. Go all the way. Be that part.

NANCY: Well, my parents betrayed me in a lot of ways. One of the tasks—

I: But we're not talking about your parents now. We're talking about a piece of you. A piece of you that says, "I want you to suffer." Be that part of you that wants you to suffer.

NANCY: I can't stay with it.

I: Nancy, it's easy to blame your parents. And I'm

not saying that they didn't contribute to your anxiety. But your parents have nothing to do with it now. Now it's you.

NANCY: Right.

I: It's you who must stand up for yourself. It's you who can make that decision. And this part of yourself has got to be confronted. You can confront this part. You've done it before. Say one sentence from that part of you, just as you did last week.

NANCY: (Very quietly) You like to suffer. It makes you feel self-righteous. It absolves you of all responsibility. It means you've been able to get away without sticking up for yourself all these years. It means you can always blame all this on somebody else. You could always start to cry. You didn't know, didn't have enough experience. It's not a good excuse anymore. It never really was. It just served its purpose so you didn't have to deal with it. So what do you do about it? Are you going to sit there and cower, or are you going to do something about it? Let's see who's gonna win this one.

I: Who is going to win this one?

NANCY: I am. I'm going to win this one.

I: Say it again.

NANCY: I'm going to win this. Ultimately I'm going to win this. It's not going to happen right away, but I will.

I: Can you feel that?

NANCY: Yeah. But I'm afraid of letting it dissipate. I'm

afraid of having to walk out of this room and lose my resolve.

I: Say it again.

NANCY: I'm gonna win this. (Shouting) I'm gonna win this!

I: Yes. Really get behind it.

NANCY: I'm winning. I don't know how, but I will.

I: You're demonstrating how. You had a tremendous victory. Absolutely tremendous. You had enormous ambivalence and you stayed with it and you won. And that's what it takes.

NANCY: You can't allow any ambivalence to stop you.

I: Right. You have to stay with it. Because it's an internal battle between two parts of yourself. There was nobody else in that battle but you and you.

You've done such brave and solid work. I hope you allow yourselves to enjoy the full measure of your victories.

THE REPEATED BATTLE is most important, and I want to emphasize it.

When we work on these psychological exercises we are in a battle between our consciousness—that is, what we want to do—and our unconscious forces that oppose us. Therefore we may regard this work as that of strengthening consciousness.

It's like body building. If we buy free weights, for example, and just look at them, we're not going to strengthen the muscle. We have to lift the weights repeatedly to create greater strength.

The same principle holds wherever we want to build new strength. In this instance we have to confront our inner adversarial voices repeatedly so that we strengthen our conscious position. Like buying the weights and merely looking at them, understanding the concept of the work—acknowledging the inner voices, even understanding how we acquired them—is of no value without the added active work of confrontation.

For this, our last workshop, I asked Steve and Nancy to review and evaluate their workshop experiences.

> STEVE: I feel pretty good about this whole thing. I know I've learned some things that I wouldn't have put together—about my dad—about how I drag him around. But better than knowing why, I know what to do with it. It's one thing to know why it's happening, it's another thing to know what to do about it when it's happening. And I feel really confident about the confrontations.

> NANCY: Well, it's funny you say that, because after our first session here I said to my husband that I realized that stage fright wasn't just about speaking in public. It also contributes to problems between us. For example, someone is renovating our kitchen and he's not doing it right and I can't confront him. I back down. And my husband, who is very forceful, can't understand it, and every time it happens he gets angry with me. And I said I realized that those situations had to do with stage fright as well. That I simply can't ask for what I deserve and insist on it and not cave in. And I'm learning, although it's hard, that I can't

miss any opportunity to stand my ground. 'Cause when I need to stand up for myself, I have to do it right then and there. And I'm really clear on that.

I: Yes, right then and there. One of the things I think you'll find if you don't is that your symptoms will start to return. When you don't express what you really want, you're reinforcing that it's dangerous to be so visible. If you miss the opportunity and that should happen, see if you can trace the anxiety back to the moment when the symptoms started—whether it's the heart that you become aware of, dry throat, (to Nancy) tearfulness, shaky voice, (to Steve) laughter, critical inner voice. Ask yourself, What did I want to do that I didn't do? What did I want to say that I didn't say? What impulse did I have to assert myself that I didn't follow?

NANCY: So if I practice standing up for myself—the things that I would have avoided in the past or not wanted to confront—do you think that the practice of doing that will help to alleviate my stage fright?

I: Enormously. You'll be reasserting your commitment to yourself to conquer this fear. The more you do that, the more this technique will work for you. Every time you can chalk up a positive, brave reaction where it would have been a negative, fearful one, you are making a different history of experience and a different expectation for the future.

Follow-up

When I checked with Steve five months later, he was doing well. He said he had had a highly emotional experience three days after the workshop ended. He had been able to acknowledge long-buried guilt over his own past misdeeds, and while this had been very painful, it had helped him to realize that he had wanted to be punished for them. This, too, he realized, contributed to his stage fright. He also felt that something within him was more open and that he was still learning. He said:

> I'm much more aware when it comes up, how it's approaching me. There are times when it catches me off guard and I forget I have something to use. But I can confront it at least 70 to 75 percent of the time. . . . The workshop put a lot of light on my relationship with my father. I never realized what an affect he had on me. I also feel okay about a lot of things I can forgive myself for—a lot of things I used to be guilty about.

Two months after the workshop ended, Nancy reported a major confrontation with a colleague she had regarded as powerful. Without inhibition, she was easily articulate and aggressive. She stood her ground.

Nancy expressed surprise at how far she had come "in such a short time."

After six months she reported:

> I'm doing better. It's still hard, but much easier than it was. Before a confrontation I say, "It doesn't matter if

they like you,'' and it works. Sometimes I don't even have to say it. In several situations, where previously I would have cried, now there's no desire or urge to cry. . . . I have a sense of pride about having successfully confronted people and gotten my way a little more. In general, I feel calmer and prouder. It's amazing.

PART TWO

Resolutions

Working on Your Own

The best way of dealing with the unconscious is the creative way. Create for instance a fantasy. Work it out with all the means at your disposal . . . as if you were it or in it, as you would work out a real situation in life which you cannot escape. —C. G. JUNG

SINCE IT IS MY BELIEF that performance anxiety is rooted in childhood experience, together we will journey back in time so you may stand with your child self and begin to come to terms with your fear. Our work may make it possible for you to learn how your pattern of anxiety became established, but even if you can't identify its source, you will come to know the images and voices that live within its boundaries. This is the energy that feeds your anxiety, and when we have completed our work together you will be able to short-circuit its power.

You may want to read this chapter in its entirety before you begin your own work. Do so if you wish, but then put aside what you have read and concentrate only on the current exercise without anticipating what lies ahead.

I included Nancy's and Steve's work in the hope that it might be useful to you when you are working on your own. (For example, you might want to refer to it for clarification of technique.) The danger in doing so, however, is that you might unconsciously imitate their processes, thinking that their outcomes are the "right" ones. There are no "right" outcomes. When you do your work your psyche will lead you wherever you need to go to confront your fear; your journey will be the result of your past experiences and your current needs.

You will notice that the format and content for your workshop differs somewhat from theirs. There are several reasons for this.

In a group setting, we use the "audience" to expose our projections. When working alone, you'll find that my questions will help you do the same thing.

I have also developed several new exercises for you to compensate for the lack of spontaneous insights that emerge as the result of group process.

Finally, though your exercises cover the same ground as Steve's and Nancy's, they have been constructed to do so without my physical presence.

When you do your own work it is especially important that you go slowly and without demand for a "result," allowing the process to work. My workshops are intense group experiences interlaced with work alone at home. Participants usually have six weeks to integrate their discoveries. No matter how much inner work you may have done in the past, do not rush your work. Whether or not introspection is new to you, your psyche will need time to digest the ideas, memories, and emotions that the exercises will unearth for you.

Rushing will be counterproductive. It will indicate a lack of respect for your own needs; it might even be a repetition of ways in which you were treated (and thus learned to treat yourself) in childhood.

Speed is no substitute for depth of experience. You will need to repeat certain exercises in order to allow yourself to open to them fully. This is not at all unusual, as you saw in Nancy's and Steve's workshop. Your intention will bring results, even if they are not visible at first.

The progression of the exercises has been constructed to allow the psyche to open slowly as its contents are invited to emerge. Do not jump over any suggested step; each step is there to help you further your own process. This will require trust on your part, and trust may be something you have in short supply. Do the best you can with the exercises, and your trust will grow as you experience your own truth emerging.

In some of the exercises I will ask you to write answers to questions as you go along; in others you will write after you have completed the exercise. In each instance your writing is a very important part of the exercise. Even though the experiences may have been powerful in the moment and will, therefore, continue to resonate within you, their conscious impact will fade unless captured on the page. Writing helps to pin them down in consciousness.

We also record as much of the content of the exercises as we can so that we may reflect on what we have experienced. When we reflect we look within, and in doing so, we become more receptive to the messages from the psyche. In this way, we not only have the experiences, we are also able to become aware of their meaning. And in later reflecting on your notes, you may find that the many threads gathered as a result of having recorded these exercises can be connected to give you a wider perspective.

Just as I participated with Nancy and Steve in their workshop, I'll be with you every step of the way as my questions stimulate your memory and emotions and my words clarify your technique and encourage you to keep going.

This work consists of two equally important parts.

One part is designed to make conscious our patterns of thinking and behavior. This is necessary, for if we are unconscious of our systems, we are powerless to change them. Toward this end, we examine our past history to try to learn how patterns may have been established. Our method is to ask questions of ourselves and write down and reflect on our answers.

Of equal importance is active engagement with our inner adversarial energy. By actively confronting the inhibiting and terrifying parts of ourselves, we weaken their power and free their energy for consciousness. With this inclusion we open the possibility for new options, thereby expanding our lives.

Steve's training as an actor was a help in his confrontations, but Nancy did just as well without that training. As you will see when you do the exercises, they will be equally effective for anyone who will allow his or her imagination to inform the work.

TIME FRAME

You will probably be able to complete the entire workshop in ten weeks, if you choose to work on these exercises for one hour once a week and use the time between sessions for inner reflection. By that time, this technique will have become sufficiently reliable for you to be able to confront your anxiety before it can escalate into panic. And if you continue to work and reflect on these exercises, you will find that your performance anxiety will continue to diminish.

Some people will want to work more frequently, and you may certainly do so if this is your preference, but do not work more often than every other day or longer than one hour at a time. The exercises are meant to stir the psyche, not to flood you with more material than you can integrate with relative comfort. You will need time to digest and integrate the material that will emerge from the exercises, for only so much can be metabolized at any given time.

If you haven't completed the entire exercise within one hour, find a place to stop, and begin where you left off the next time you work.

If you finish an exercise with time to spare, use the remainder of the hour to reflect on what the exercise has produced.

When you have completed an exercise, allow at least one day for further reflection and integration of new material before going on to the next exercise.

The time off is important. Don't skip it no matter how eager you may be to forge ahead.

SUGGESTIONS FOR SUCCESS

One of the ways in which you can ensure success is by protecting and honoring your commitment to yourself to do this work.

Make your workshop an appointment with yourself, note it on your calendar, and keep the appointment. Treat it as an appointment with someone you value highly and are eager to meet.

Your preparation for each workshop is important. It will free you to keep the focus on your inner processes and should be completed before you begin each exercise.

Provide a quiet, private place for yourself—the same place each time you do the work. This will become a nurturing, safe environment for you, and being there will help you to relax and open to the unconscious and its messages.

Decide to begin at a certain time on a certain day, and determine (and protect) the times that are best for your subsequent work. Be realistic about your choices so that you will be able to have the quiet and privacy you will need. Choose times when you are alone and are not likely to be intruded upon by the needs or demands of roommates, spouses, or children.

Wear loose, comfortable clothing so that any physical discomfort you experience while doing an exercise may be clearly attributable to your anxiety and not to your clothing.

Turn off the phone.

Set an alarm clock for one hour so you can forget about time.

Have a blanket available in case you become cold. It is important that you learn to recognize and respond to your physical needs.

Have a notebook and pen at hand. When working alone, you have no outside witness to validate your courage, no "other" to reaffirm your discoveries. By notating the material that is evoked by the exercises, you will be able to become your own witness as you revisit what has occurred.

It will not be possible to remember everything that occurs

during the exercises, so do not make that a goal. In having had the experiences, you will have gained something of value, which will leave its mark within you even if you don't consciously remember all of it afterward. Just do the best you can.

If you smoke, please do without your cigarettes while you are working on these exercises. People often reach for a cigarette when they are feeling anxious, and doing so may help you to relieve your tension and bury feelings and memories that want to surface. This is counterproductive; we are trying to release feelings and emotions—not bury them.

For the same reason, I suggest not drinking coffee or tea or chewing gum during the exercises.

As you begin each exercise, carefully read it in its entirety so that you will be familiar with the questions and directions that it contains. Do not let the number of steps in the exercises put you off. These are meant to create a structure for you, to prod your feelings and memories, not to restrict you. If you deviate somewhat from the written form, follow the psyche's lead. You will have other opportunities to do the exercises as written, and the outlines are meant only to support your work.

DEALING WITH RESISTANCE

Resistance is not wrong or bad. It is a means of self-defense. It is not an accident that we react the way we do. Your fear was once aimed at keeping you protected. Since we are dealing with habits that are old and deeply ingrained, do not expect to give up this mode of self-protection without reluctance. Your fear response will not change unless and until something within you becomes convinced that it is safe for you to come out of hiding.

Resistance can come in many forms.

You may make the decision to go ahead, but then, at the time you've set aside for this work, meet with resistance in the form of something "important" that must be attended to immediately.

Or, you may begin the work and then experience loss of concentration, boredom, or lack of confidence that the technique will work for you.

Or, you may unconsciously invite people to invade your privacy with their needs.

Or, you may be led repeatedly to a place of trauma and be tempted to judge or inhibit your exploration by labeling it "repetitious." The same incident may require repeated exploration. This can be seen clearly in Nancy's work with her inner child, as each encounter took her process further and deeper.

Or, you may be reluctant to devote so much time and energy to yourself, labeling it selfish or self-centered.

You can help to neutralize your resistance by remembering what your fear cost you.

Here's an easy and effective exercise for dealing with resistance.

OVERCOMING RESISTANCE

1. Remember a time when the price you paid for your anxiety was particularly high.

2. Did you have a good idea that you didn't dare to express?

3. Did you want publicly to offer a toast to someone you love?

4. Were you too afraid to go after a much-wanted job? Accept the first such memory that occurs to you now.

5. Allow yourself to remember the experience in detail.

6. What happened (or didn't happen) during the event?

7. Afterward, how did you feel?

8. And now, how do you feel about spending the rest of your life with this disorder?

As much as we say, and believe, we want to change, there is a pull to repeat the past because we have been conditioned to do so. By recognizing resistance when it arises, and acknowledging it as "normal," we can move through it.

Many people for whom this technique ultimately worked well announced at our first workshop meeting that they hated being there and came only out of desperation.

You, too, may have misgivings about opening yourself to this process. It's okay to hate the idea of the work, as long as you do it anyway. Your attempt to open to the psyche will bring results even if they are barely visible at first. Stay with it and give yourself a chance to see how well this technique can work for you.

DEALING WITH ANXIETY
AROUSED BY THE EXERCISES

These exercises are meant to stir memories and emotions, to make you more conscious of how you felt when you were a child and how you feel now.

Since we will be taking you back to the origins of your fear, expect to experience some anxiety as you do the exercises. Unlike performance anxiety experienced in the outer world, anxiety in your private room will produce nothing more dire than discomfort, for there will be no one—except you—whose opinion of you might be affected by your anxiety. If you do berate yourself for what you experience during the exercises, record this in your notebook, and you will see how devoted you are to undermining your own efforts.

The knowledge that you have brought this anxiety on deliberately should make it bearable. But if it becomes too great, return to Exercise #1, the Relaxation Exercise. It will calm and center you and help you to feel in control again. Knowing you have this safety net will make it easier for you to try again.

Remember, we are deliberately stimulating your anxiety so that you can explore it and learn as much as possible about it. *You are inviting your anxiety to manifest in this safe private place so that you will no longer be helpless when it strikes you in the everyday world.*

EXPECTATIONS

It is natural to want results from your work. However, just as people cannot be sufficiently objective to analyze their own dreams, people also cannot evaluate the "success" of these exercises.

Try not to burden your work with expectations.

Follow each direction, and work to do exercises as fully as possible rather than for a specific result.

Allow each new experience to bring whatever it may. If you compare what you perceive to be today's result with what you thought was yesterday's, you will subvert the process.

If you are like most people with performance anxiety, a part of you is critical and perfectionistic. Don't allow that part to interfere with your effort.

Perfection is not our goal.

Your effort will open access to the psyche; your effort will bring results.

WHERE TO BEGIN

In everyday life, we fight for the illusion of control over our environment. When we do our inner work, we ask ourself to give up that attempt at control and allow our inner partner to influence what we think and feel. But until we are comfortable dealing with the unconscious, we need a transitional pathway from outer behavior to receptivity to the inner life. This is created by the Relaxation Exercise.

In deep relaxation we quiet the outer noise, thereby allowing our self to hear and feel what is happening within. Early in your work at home, you will find it helpful always to begin with the Relaxation Exercise. After you have become familiar with listening for your inner child

(Exercises #5 and #6), you may no longer need to use the exercise as a bridge. You may also find that you can more easily call forth your inner voices after you become willing to hear them.

Now, as you begin this work, even if you think you do not need it, do the Relaxation Exercise.

Exercise 1: Relaxation Exercise

Wear loose, comfortable clothing and remove your shoes.

Make sure you will not be disturbed.

Turn off the phone.

At the time you have selected, go to your quiet private place.

Set your alarm clock for one hour.

Turn down the lights.

Have a notebook and pen handy.

Sit on a chair or lie down.

Be physically comfortable. If you're cold, cover yourself with a blanket.

In the group workshops, when doing the Relaxation Exercise, I give directions to participants in a quiet, unhurried voice. You will need to do this for yourself at home, addressing yourself in thought in the same way. Or you may find it helpful to record the following instructions so you may listen to your own voice gently giving yourself permission to let go of tension, of holding, as you find it in the body.

TECHNIQUE

Allow your eyelids to close.

(Then slowly ask yourself to do the following:)

Feel the chair or floor beneath you. Give yourself over to the chair or floor as fully as you can; allow it to support you.

(Allow a moment for this to occur before going on.)

Concentrate on your breathing for a few moments. Without demand, observe the process as you inhale and exhale.

(Pause after each of the following instructions, allowing yourself time to follow each one.)

Now, continuing your quiet breathing, place all your concentration on your toes and allow them to release.

Now go into the balls of your feet and release.

Now your arches and release.

Your heels and release.

Now go back and slowly check each foot to see that it is released from holding.

If you find any places of tension, release them by breathing into them.

Now go into your ankles and release.

Your calves and release.

(Check from time to time to see that the relaxation remains in areas already covered.)

Continue in this way until you have let go of tension in your entire body, ending with your face and head.

(If you find tension in your jaw, your release might bring a sound with it, an audible exhalation, or your mouth might fall open as the hinge beside your ears is allowed to let go.)

Go through your body as slowly and methodically as you can, allowing (not demanding) yourself to let go of tension as you find it. The tension is not "wrong" or "bad," it is just the way in which you are holding yourself. Release can also be learned. If, after breathing into a place of tension, release is difficult for you, increase the tension in this place to its maximum and then release it. This exaggeration will help you recognize what may be a more subtle pattern of holding of which you have been unaware.

If you have habitually removed your consciousness from your body in an effort to escape its pain, being so fully present in the body may feel foreign or even threatening to you. If you become very anxious during the exercise, return to concentrating on your breathing before going on.

Do not rush this process. Allow yourself to do the exercise as slowly as necessary, remaining in any area as long as necessary, giving yourself the time you need to relax.

Your mind will be busy and wander or flit from subject to subject. Observe the activity for a moment, allowing it without judgment, and gently return your attention to your breathing and relaxation.

Stay with the exercise and feel, finally, what it is like to be in a quiet, peaceful body. If you are unfamiliar with this feeling of relaxation, this may take some practice.

If you are habitually hypervigilant, it may not be easy to let go. Perhaps it is even too difficult to keep your eyes closed while you do the exercise. This is not wrong—there is no "wrong" way to do the exercise. Your task is simply to do the best you can. You will use this exercise repeatedly in conjunction with other exercises, so you will have plenty of opportunities to practice it, and within a short time you will be able to identify and release tension quickly.

Falling asleep before completing the exercise may indicate resistance to going further due to anxiety. This is not something for which to berate yourself—it is only your fear reasserting itself. Try again and stay with the exercise as long as you can. Ultimately you will be able to complete it. You might also find it helpful to choose an earlier time for the exercise.

If you fall asleep after you have completed the exercise, enjoy it. Your clock will wake you when the hour is over, and you will awaken refreshed.

Stay with this exercise for the entire hour.

At the end of the hour, wiggle your toes and slowly move your arms and legs. Stretch and open your eyes. Allow a few moments for your awareness to come back into the room. Engage in some quiet activity before you attempt to return to your usual tempo.

If you are unused to deep relaxation, you may find that emotions and memories arise merely from letting go of tension. (In fact, your tension may have been designed to enable you to control your emotions.) If emotions or thoughts do arise, write down whatever comes to you, for it will in some way be related to your anxiety. Your psyche knows the aim of your work and will produce material to help you in your journey toward greater freedom from fear.

Exercise 2: Probing for Memories of Childhood

In this exercise you will be asked to answer a series of questions pertaining to your childhood. This is not a test, and there is no way to come up with "wrong" answers. If you change your mind about one of your answers, that will be fine. But don't erase anything you've written: merely add the new answers. Contradictions are valuable and may be used to learn about confusion or conflict. Let all your answers stand so that you can review them at a later time. Remember, do not spend more than one hour on your workshop.

You will use your notebook and pen during this exercise.

It is important that you spend a few minutes on each of the following questions, allowing time for memories, emotions, and feelings to return to you.

Remain with each memory and each answer until you feel it is complete at this time. For example, if you have a memory of a particular occurrence with one of your parents, remain with that memory and do not switch to a different one during the exercise. On subsequent occasions you will have time to explore other memories, and flitting from one scene to another may be unconsciously designed to keep your memory superficial so as to lessen the impact of old wounds. Do not attack yourself if it is difficult for you to stay with a memory. It is natural to want to avoid pain.

"Yes" or "No" are not adequate answers. "I don't remember" is an acceptable initial answer, as long as you think about the question until you do remember.

Work on one question at a time, writing your answers as

fully as you can before going on. If something occurs to you after you have completed an answer, add it.

TECHNIQUE

1. Complete the Relaxation Exercise, taking no more than ten minutes to do so.

After you have completed the exercise and are relaxed, allow yourself to think back to childhood, and ask yourself the following questions:

2. Did my parents support my individuality?
3. Did they encourage me to speak my mind?
4. Did they welcome my opinions?
5. Was I praised when I was daring?
6. Was I told how proud they were of me?
7. Was I told how smart they thought I was?

Perhaps you are now remembering a particular day or occurrence. Stay with this memory, and enter it in your notebook. Please continue with the exercise.

8. Was it all right with my parents for me to be different from the rest of the family?
9. Was it all right with my parents for me to be quiet?
10. Were my parents, more often than not, critical of me and my ideas?
11. My talents?
12. My aspirations?
13. Was I made to feel that I was a disappointment to my parents unless I excelled?
14. Were my parents hard to please?
15. Was I pushed to make them proud of me?

16. Was I led to understand that my being seen and heard was unwelcome to them?

17. What made me feel this way?

18. Was I punished a great deal?

19. In what ways?

20. How did I feel about this?

21. In what ways did their punishment have an impact on the way I felt about myself?

22. How do I feel about this now?

23. How do I feel about asking myself these questions?

If there is still time remaining to your hour, keep thinking about the questions and writing down your answers. We write our answers to pin them down so that we may reflect on them and add to them as memories return.

If you find supportive, encouraging memories of child-hood in response to these questions, this is valuable, too. We are trying to find the roots of your performance anxiety, and everything that we learn about you is of value.

Now, give yourself time to come back into everyday reality as you return to the outer world.

Continue to reflect on these questions and your answers until your next session.

Exercise 3: Evoking the Past

This exercise taps into one of the psyche's commonly experienced means of self-expression—the dramas we call dreams. We readily accept the appearance of people in our dreams, and though we call it by another name, we do the same thing while we are awake—only now we call it a daydream or a fantasy.

Now we will create a fantasy without having any goal as to its outcome. The psyche can be counted on to lead you where you need to go, as it did with Nancy and Steve when they worked on this same exercise.

Complete your preparation for your inner work.

Have your notebook and pen handy.

TECHNIQUE

1. Complete the Relaxation Exercise, taking about ten minutes to do so.

2. Now slowly stand, giving yourself time to adjust to being on your feet, and say your first name aloud repeatedly, as if you are calling yourself.

This may feel strange at first, but it is important that you use your voice along with your imagination for these exercises.

3. As you call yourself, allow yourself to feel whatever may arise.

4. Give yourself over to the exercise as completely as you can.

5. Allow your feelings, emotions, and memories to surface as much as you can, but do not allow them to interfere with your calling your name.

6. Allow variations on your name, should they evolve.

For example, you may begin with "Elizabeth, Elizabeth, Elizabeth, Elizabeth, Elizabeth, Lizzie, Lizzie, Lizzie, Elizabeth, Elizabeth, Lizzie, Liz, Lizzie, Beth, Beth, Lizzie," etc. etc.

If your mind wanders far afield and the exercise feels flat, gently bring it back to what you are doing and continue to call your name without judging the result. There is a difference between a mind that wanders because of fear and one that takes you to fertile territory. When the wanderings are dictated by fear and the desire to escape your feelings, the exercises feel dead; when the territory is fertile, something opens in the psyche, and the exercises feel alive.

7. Stay with the exercise by repeatedly calling your name, and give it a chance to work for you.

Again, we are not looking for a particular result. We are opening a pathway to the unconscious so that your individual material may emerge. Whatever comes for you is the "right" thing; this is your psyche's response to your work. It is assisting you in the best way that it can.

In your mind's eye, if a person appears who seems to be the one calling your name:

8. Be specific in seeing him or her.

9. Who is he or she?

10. How does it feel now to see him or her?

11. What is your relationship to him or her?

12. How does he or she look?

13. Listen to his/her tone of voice.

14. How does he or she sound?

15. Does the caller's tone of voice evoke any feelings in you?

16. Can you allow yourself to acknowledge and express these feelings?

17. Does this exercise evoke memories involving this caller?

18. How are you affected by this experience right now?

19. Is there anything familiar in this experience and in the ways in which you are reacting to this caller?

20. If you can do so, and want to do so, answer the caller.

21. In the event that you and the caller want to talk with each other, you can do so.

In your imagination, you can slip into the image of the caller and imbue him or her with the ability to talk with you. Age is no obstacle, nor is gender. Just as Steve, in his exercises, was a female schoolteacher as well as his father, in your fantasy you can "be" either male or female with equal ease. Children do this all the time. Once you did, too. Just give yourself permission to go ahead, and you will easily do so.

You may find, in "being" the caller, that you experience unfamiliar feelings that belong to him or her. Let them influence the tone of voice and attitude of the caller. Allow these feelings to fully express themselves now.

If this exercise has taken you back to childhood, perhaps the child you once were will also come forward in your imagination.

You can now slip into this child, infusing it with life, just as you did the caller and just as Nancy did with her three-year-old self. All that is necessary is for you to permit your imagination to lead you.

22. Allow the pictures in your mind to unfold without judgment, giving life to each figure as it emerges, following and participating with each of them as fully as you can.

23. Give yourself over to your fantasy. Fantasy is closely

related to dreaming; like dreaming, it is the product of the unconscious. Again, it is your psyche's response to what it knows is your attempt to confront your performance anxiety.

24. Again, allow yourself to experience your feelings as fully as you can. When the dialogue becomes repetitious or when it no longer feels alive, say good-bye to your inner characters as if they were real people. If you wish, tell them you will return to them and that they can come to you whenever they like.

25. Immediately after the exercise, write down as much of the dialogue and your feelings as you can remember, along with your reactions to this experience. You will not be able to remember everything that happened.

If, while doing the exercise, you do not receive any memory, image, or feeling, and you have repeatedly called your name for five minutes (which will feel like a very long time), leave it for today and return to the Relaxation Exercise. The next time you work, begin again with the Relaxation Exercise and then return to this exercise. You may have to do this several times before you are relaxed enough for something to come to you. Do not go on to the next exercise until you have experienced the caller as a real person from your past.

If this is difficult for you, don't despair. Resistance is greater in some exercises than in others, and this will just be a momentary obstruction in your journey. I have never known the exercise to fail to produce a caller, as long as it was given enough time.

If you feel it would be helpful, refer to the Steve and

Nancy chapter, where you will find examples of what this exercise brought to them. I suggest this only to clarify technique, not in any way to imply that your outcome will be the same as theirs.

Again, even if you have completed the exercise, wait at least one day before going on. During that time allow yourself to reflect on the exercise and acknowledge what it brought you. Also review what you have written in your notebook.

Now give yourself time to come back into everyday reality.

Exercise 4: Identifying Your Inner Critic

This exercise consists of a group of questions pertaining to your attitudes about yourself. It is not a test and there are no "wrong" answers.

Change into comfortable clothing and complete your preparation for your inner work.

Consider the following questions, taking your time with each and writing down your answers as you go along. "I don't know" is acceptable as an initial response, provided you stay with the question until you come up with an answer that evokes more feeling.

Allowing memories, emotions, and feelings to surface will help you to answer these questions. If you are unable to answer any question, come back to it later.

Write down as many answers to each question as you can, and add to them as memories return.

Again, you have a whole hour, so really take the time to think about each question.

———— ■ ————

TECHNIQUE

1. Complete the Relaxation Exercise, spending no more than ten minutes to do so. When you are relaxed, ask yourself the following questions:

2. How critical am I of myself?

3. How often do I put myself down?

4. How forgiving am I of my mistakes?

5. Now recall your last experience of performance anxiety.

Use the first example that comes to mind and stay with that occurrence.

Be specific in your memory.

6. In your imagination, take yourself to the place where you experienced this attack of performance anxiety.

7. Walk into the room in your mind's eye.

8. See the people who are there.

9. Who are they?

10. What is your relationship to them?

11. How do you feel about them?

12. What do you want from them?

13. What is at stake for you on this occasion?

14. In your imagination, begin to speak to them.

15. What is happening to you physically?

16. Identify your physical symptoms in minute detail, writing them down (such as, "My heart is pounding in my ears, I want to run, I can't swallow," etc.).

17. How do you feel emotionally?

Identify as many feelings as you can, writing them down.

18. What are your judgments of yourself for having these anxiety symptoms?

Take your time and really explore your judgments, writing them down.

19. Now, imagine that a dear friend is having these same symptoms.

20. What are your judgments toward your friend for having these anxiety symptoms?

21. Do you find that there is a difference in your judgments when the symptoms are yours as opposed to when they're your friend's?

22. If so, what's the difference?

23. If so, toward whom are you more sympathetic?

24. Is there anything familiar in the way you are judging yourself?

25. Give yourself time to consider if it is possible that in these judgments you are now judging yourself as you were judged in childhood.

26. From now on, try to become aware of circumstances where you automatically feel you have to be careful and hide your true reactions, when you feel you have to be pleasing rather than real.

Write down what you discover, and keep adding to your list.

Give yourself time to come back into everyday reality.

Reflect on this exercise until your next session. You will

also find it profitable to review what you have written in response to these exercises.

Allow at least one day before going to the next exercise.

Exercise 5: Contacting Your Inner Child

If the concept of an inner life is a relatively unfamiliar one, you will need to learn to listen for the inner voices that you may customarily override in your everyday life.

We all have these voices. They are communication from the unconscious part of the psyche, and as such they are a part of us.

You may be coming to realize that you felt endangered in childhood. You may be remembering why you believed that being seen and heard was dangerous. If so, you may now see that you have gone into hiding even from yourself.

It is important that we now puncture this old inhibiting belief system so that you can come out of hiding.

You can learn to listen for the feelings that frequently come into our minds as "voices," by acknowledging that something within you is saying, "I feel bad, I feel frightened, I feel angry," or sad, lost, and the like.

I conceptualize this exercise as listening to the inner child because I believe that it was your childhood inability to respond honestly to insult or injury that helped set the pattern for your performance anxiety. So it is to this child, still young and alive in the psyche, that we must return for its healing.

Change into comfortable clothing, and complete your preparation for your inner work.

TECHNIQUE

1. Complete the Relaxation Exercise. You may now be able to do so in less than ten minutes.

2. From this relaxed place, visualize yourself as a child.

Accept the first picture of yourself that comes into your head. This choice is not a casual one but is chosen by something within you and indicates that there is a connection between the child in your fantasy and your performance anxiety.

3. Let this child come alive for you.

Really see this child in as much detail as possible as a living child.

Is it smiling?

Crying?

Angry?

Happy?

Hurt?

Frightened?

4. How do you feel about this child as it appears to you now?

5. Would you like to embrace this child?

6. Take it on your lap?

7. If so, do so in your imagination.

Be specific in your fantasy. Really allow yourself to feel the weight of this child on your lap.

8. Does this evoke feelings in you?

9. Allow yourself to express them.

10. What are the child's feelings?

11. Can you allow them to be expressed?

12. If so, do so.

13. Are you holding anything back?

14. If so, can you allow yourself to express *anything* more fully?

15. Do you want to talk to this child?

16. If so, do so.

17. Does this child want to say or do something?

18. If so, allow it to do so. (Even if the child is an infant, allow it to express its feelings in words.)

19. Allow the fantasy to take you where it wishes.

If you feel unsympathetic toward the child, allow yourself to express this as fully as you can without judgment.

Take the time to be specific in your answers.

20. How do you feel about this child?

21. What do you want to do with this child now?

22. Do so in your imagination.

23. How do you and the child feel about this?

24. How does the child feel about you?

25. Ask the child if it has anything it wants to express to you.

26. Do you want to allow the child to express itself?

27. If so, do so.

28. If not, why not?

29. Talk to the child if you wish to do so.

30. Keep the dialogue going as you would in reality.

There is no "correct" outcome to this exercise. You are merely learning to contact your inner child. Stay with the child as long as it wants to stay with you. That is, be guided by the needs of this child who was, and remains, a part of you.

When the energy diminishes or the dialogue becomes repetitious, it is time to leave the exercise.

31. Say good-bye to the child and tell her or him that you will return.

32. If you wish, you may add that the child can come to you whenever it wants, that you want to be available to its needs, that you want to have it in your life.

———————————————————————

Immediately after the exercise, write down as much of the dialogue and your experience as you can. Don't expect to remember everything that happened. Just record as much as you can, and keep what you have written.

Again, please take the time to be specific in identifying what you see and feel.

While there is no right or wrong way to do this exercise, it can be subverted by being careful, by insisting that it be logical, by judging your outcome, or by inhibiting reactions that you consider "shameful" or "not nice."

Try to stay with the exercise, but if you are not able to do so for any reason, go back to the Relaxation Exercise and spend the remainder of your time with that. At the end of the hour, write down anything that came to you even if it feels vague or incomplete.

Remember, everything that has ever happened to you has left its mark within the psyche. Everything, even if you no longer remember it on a conscious plane, continues to have an effect on your life.

You can gain access to your precious psychic material by doing this work.

Remember also:

If you habitually put down or deny your feelings and

reactions, if you think you always have to appear "good" or "kind," you might not like what emerges from these exercises, but take a chance and be honest and see what you might learn from them.

If you stay with the process, something will appear for you.

Do not demand the same result each time you do an exercise. There is no "correct" result.

Whatever you get is in some way related to your performance anxiety and is a gift from your unconscious.

At the end of the hour, allow yourself time to come back into everyday reality.

Reflect on the material that emerged until your next session.

Exercise 6: Revisiting Your Inner Child

Repeat Exercise #5, Contacting Your Inner Child, beginning as always with the Relaxation Exercise. You may receive a similar fantasy, or it may be a different one. Either way is fine.

After you have completed the exercise, again write down your experience in as much detail as you are able.

If you are unable to repeat the exercise, return to the Relaxation Exercise and remain with it for the hour. Try again the next time you do the work.

When you have completed this exercise twice, you may go on to the next exercise during your next session, if you feel ready to do so.

If you feel unable to absorb any more information at this time, respect your needs and adjust your work schedule so that you can have more time to integrate the material unearthed by these exercises.

Remember, going on before you are ready to do so does not produce faster or more profound results.

You have now completed over half of the exercises.

Are you more conscious of your attitudes about yourself?

Are you aware of any changes in your self-judgments?

Are there any differences in the way you interact with others?

Add these insights to the material in your notebook.

If this is the first time you have done inner journeying, I hope you are finding it as interesting and valuable as I and others do. These explorations of your psyche will widen your consciousness so that your life will expand. And as we proceed you will see how the techniques you have been learning can be employed to confront your performance anxiety.

But first, take the time now to allow yourself to feel the deep satisfaction that comes from working to free your true self.

Exercise 7: Examining an Attack of Performance Anxiety

These questions are designed to stimulate further thinking about your performance anxiety and the role it plays in your life.

In this instance, work on two consecutive days, if you can, spending one hour each day. If you are unable to answer any question during the first day, go on with the exercise and return to the unanswered question on the second day. Then allow at least one day for rest, reflection, and integration before going on.

Give yourself time to answer each question. "I don't know" is all right as an initial answer, as long as you continue to struggle with the question until you do come up with an answer. Again, there are no right or wrong answers. If you have not been able to answer all the questions, try to do so the next time you work.

When you're in the midst of a panic attack, there's not much you can do except get through it. But after the fact there is something you can do to help yourself.

Afterward you can go over the experience in minute detail, asking yourself the following questions and writing down your answers as fully as you can.

From now on, as soon as you can after you have an episode of performance anxiety, go to your private place and do this exercise.

In preparation for this exercise now:

Change into comfortable clothing and prepare your room for your inner work.

Give yourself time to consider each answer and write down your answers as you go along.

TECHNIQUE

1. Complete the Relaxation Exercise. This may take extra resolve if you are still flooded with the adrenaline

produced in your brain's response to fear. Perhaps you can do so in five or six minutes.

2. Call to mind your last attack of performance anxiety. This may create anxiety for you now, but you can keep it from interfering with the exercise if you keep bringing your intention back to the task at hand.

3. What was your expectation of your "audience's" (boss, professional group, friends, spouse) reaction to you?

4. Was your expectation borne out in reality?

5. On this occasion, was the "audience" in fact hostile, judgmental, ready to laugh or ridicule?

6. In what way did they express this in reality?

7. If they were hostile, is this your usual experience of them?

8. Were you able to acknowledge their true reception of you?

9. How did you relate to them?

Frequently we re-create the parent-child interaction by unconsciously choosing friends, partners, or employers who will treat us the way we were treated by our parents. That is, as adults we choose important others who will respond to our needs and reactions in the same ways our parents did when we were children.

If, in fact, the boss, friend, partner, or spouse is hostile and judgmental:

10. Have you repeatedly chosen similar bosses, friends, partners, spouses?

11. Could these choices be a replay of childhood, with the boss, friend, partner, or spouse re-creating the role of your parent(s) and with you relating to the person as if you were still a child?

If the answers to the last two questions are "yes," ask yourself the following:

12. Do I want this energy in my life?
13. If not, can I do something about it?
14. Am I willing to do something about it?

You may not be able to answer this last question right now, especially if this is the first time you've encountered many of these ideas. But if these questions touched something in the way you look at yourself and your anxiety, keep asking them and eventually you will learn from your answers.

If there was no objective reason for your fear—in other words, if the "audience" was not hostile and your fear is from inner rather than outer causes—then acknowledge this fact without self-judgment. Don't beat yourself up for having reacted with anxiety.

You are not a fool, and this is not silly or "crazy," nor does it mean that you are "going crazy" or that you are weak or self-indulgent. This anxiety is not something that you can just will yourself to get over, or you would. This is not simple stage fright, and that's why conventional methods, such as deep breathing and thorough preparation, are ineffective against it.

You may be unconsciously re-creating your childhood experiences. In other words, you may have been conditioned by experiences in your childhood to expect ill treatment from "important" others.

These exercises are meant to stir up memories and to release emotions, and they may be disturbing. You may be ambivalent about proceeding. You may think my questions silly or annoying. You may even be angry with me for asking them.

That is understandable if you've been prevented (or have prevented yourself) from acknowledging what you feel. These exercises, because of their intention, may be going against a lifetime of denial and self-silencing.

But acknowledged or not, repressed feelings do not go away; rather, they grow in intensity as we reinforce them with each new repression.

As much as we may hate our liabilities, we know them, we are used to them, they may even have served a purpose in the past and may continue to do so now. This may be difficult to accept because having performance anxiety is so limiting, so embarrassing.

But be honest with yourself.

Go very slowly now, allowing your truth to emerge, writing down your answers as they come to you, and examining them to see if you can add anything more.

Ask yourself:

15. Do I really want to get rid of my fear?

This question might seem foolish to you, but it is not. Your immediate response might be a resounding "Yes," but this might not be your only answer. Allow yourself to consider the possibility that "Yes" may cover deeper layers of feelings.

16. Is it possible that I am getting something out of being so afraid?

17. What might I be getting out of being so afraid?

Many of us with performance anxiety have fantasies of how our lives would change if only we weren't so afraid of expressing our gifts and intelligence. In these fantasies we are easily articulate, accomplished, and acclaimed.

But what if you didn't have this impediment and your fantasies still didn't come true?

18. Is it possible that your anxiety attacks protect you from having to face what might be the limitations of your gifts?

19. Is it possible that your performance anxiety allows you to retain your dreams of glory?

20. Somewhere, would you rather keep your performance anxiety than risk the reality that you might not be as gifted and impressive as you are in your fantasies?

If perfection is your only acceptable standard for yourself—and this is so for most of us who suffer from performance anxiety—then imagine what it would be like to have to accept that your gifts fall short of perfection.

In other words, in a belief system where there is either perfection or abject failure—and nothing in between—anything less than perfect would be contemptible.

Please ask yourself:

21. How would I feel if it turned out that my gifts were less than I fantasize them to be?

22. Am I able to value myself if my gifts are less than extraordinary?

23. Is it possible that my fantasies of enormous success are too precious to risk losing?

———————————— ▬ ————————————

Allow yourself to reflect on what you have discovered.

Exercise 8: What Might I Be Getting from My Fear?

Begin with your preparation for your work.

TECHNIQUE

1. Complete your Relaxation Exercise, taking five minutes to do so.

2. Think about your fear.

3. Are you connected with family members or friends through your fear and the limitations it imposes on you?

4. In what ways? (Remember, "I don't know" is not an acceptable answer.)

5. Would it alter your relationship with someone of importance to you if you became less fearful and more outspoken?

6. How might things change?

7. What might you lose?

8. Would it upset the family dynamic if you weren't so frightened? (For example, does your fear provide your family with a focal point? Does it create a distraction from the problems of others? Does it "normalize" the fear of others?)

9. Does your anxiety keep you from growing up and leaving home? (This may be so even if you have physically moved away from the family home long ago.)

Now really take the time to be specific in your answers and probe as deeply as you can.

10. How would my relationship to myself change if I weren't so frightened?

11. How would my relationship to others change if I weren't so frightened?

12. How would my life change if I weren't so afraid?

13. Do I welcome these changes?

14. Am I being honest and realistic?

Keep thinking about these questions and your answers.

If you need another day to complete these two exercises, take it. Remember, by following the demands of your own inner needs, you are respecting yourself.

After you have completed Exercises #7 and #8, make sure to allow time for reflection and integration of new ideas before you go on to the next exercise.

Exercise 9: Re-creating Performance Anxiety

Those of us who suffer from performance anxiety unconsciously believe that being the center of attention is terribly dangerous. The attacks of anxiety and panic we experience when we are the focus of others' attention reinforce this conviction. The pattern of denying and trying to hide our reactions to what we perceive as danger, adopted (perhaps with good cause) in childhood, is part of the problem.

Acknowledging our physical symptoms during an anxiety attack helps to neutralize the impact of what we interpret as our body's betrayal of us.

In this exercise you will take yourself into an imaginary

experience of presenting your ideas to an audience. The more fully you give yourself to the fantasy, the more potent the exercise will be. Here the task is to go into your evoked material, not to complete your presentation, as you would feel compelled to do in everyday life.

Complete your preparation for your inner work.

Place an empty chair facing you for use as "audience" during this exercise.

After you have completed the exercise, write down your answers to these questions, along with any other feelings evoked by this exercise.

TECHNIQUE

1. Complete the Relaxation Exercise, spending no more than five minutes to do so.

2. Remember a time when something important was at stake for you—you had to give a presentation or you wanted to express an idea or display a talent—and you had an attack of anxiety.

3. Accept the first memory that comes into your mind, and stay with this memory.

Again, be specific.

4. Allow yourself to go back to that time and place, to the moments prior to your attempt at self-expression.

5. "See" your audience.

6. What is your relationship to them?

7. Does one person emerge as more dominant than the others?

8. What is your relationship to this person?

9. Now imagine this person—or, if there is no specific person, then imagine someone of importance to you—sitting in the empty chair.

10. Stand and present your material aloud to them. Make the experience as real for yourself as you can.

11. Observe the changes in your body.

12. What are they?

If you have allowed this fantasy to become real, you are probably experiencing what you have felt in reality in similar situations.

In life, when we have these symptoms, we try to hide them from our audience and we lose our concentration.

Here it is safe for you to take the time to stand and investigate your panic. Now we will deliberately concentrate on your symptoms.

13. Let your symptom have their full expression.

Do not continue with your presentation at this time but, rather, focus on your physical feelings, allowing them to expand, to become as big as they want to be.

I know this can be frightening, but stay with it. There is nothing at stake now, nothing to lose, no one to judge you but yourself.

14. Can you embody one of the manifestations of your panic? If you feel taken over by the pounding in your heart, can you allow yourself the illusion that this pounding is expanding, and can you then "be" this pounding? That is, can you allow your body and behavior to express this pounding? For instance, you might find that you begin to move your arms and feet in a percussive way, or you might gallop around your room, or you might make sounds that express what your heart is doing. Find your own way to express the pounding in your heart.

Do not judge the result of your efforts, just go along with your choice as completely as you can.

15. When this choice no longer feels alive, leave it and return to your presentation. Again, "see" the "audience," and make the presentation as real as possible.

16. What is happening to you now?

17. Tune in to your body and feelings, and see if you can allow them to take on the characteristics of a known or unknown adult or child.

Just as you "were" your heart's pounding, so can you "be" anyone or anything else in your imagination.

18. Now "be" the person who has emerged, imbuing that person with vitality, and walk around in his/her skin.

19. How does it feel to be that person?

20. Increase whatever you are doing until you experience the essence of this person.

21. Or perhaps what has emerged suggests the essence of an animal.

22. Allow yourself to "be" this animal.

For example, how does it move? How does it hold its head? What motivates it? Is it looking for something? Does it want to do something?

23. Is some form of communication possible between you and the person or animal?

24. If so, allow it, playing both parts as you have done before in other exercises.

25. Does this person or animal want something of you?

26. If so, what is it?

27. Can you give it?

28. If this person or animal wants to give something to you, can you receive it?

The feelings and images that came to you during your

presentation are part of the energy in your panic. By expanding and feeling your way into these aspects of yourself, and by experiencing them fully instead of doing everything in your power to keep them away or hidden, you are learning about yourself. You may even find that you reconnect with long denied feelings in your body or with long buried memories.

By acknowledging the existence of this newly mined energy, you move it out of the unconscious, where it has been an obstruction, into consciousness, where it can become productive, where it can increase your appetite for life.

Afterward don't forget to record your answers and as much as you can of your experience. And take the time you need to readjust before you return to everyday reality.

During your days off, reread and reflect on your notations.

A few words about physical symptoms of panic.

Many people who have performance anxiety confuse their bodies' reaction to excitement with its reaction to fear.

Can you differentiate between the two? Or do you automatically become alarmed every time your heartbeat quickens (to mention but one of the symptoms of anxiety)?

Performance anxiety is not the only cause of elevated heartbeat, trembling limbs, buzzing in one's head, and the like.

Joy can do it, too.

The next time you begin to be aware of any of these symptoms, check to determine the cause. It may not indicate the onset of anxiety.

Exercise 10: Confronting Your Inner Critic

By now you have become more aware of the voices in your head that make negative comments to you in circumstances where you feel yourself seen and heard by others. (They probably attack you even in anticipation of such events.) In this exercise you will have a confrontation with these inner voices.

Complete your preparation for your inner work.

You will need two chairs for this exercise.

Record your experience after you have completed the exercise.

During the confrontation you can differentiate an inner voice from your more conscious one by designating one of the chairs as your own and putting "the inner voice" in the other. When you are expressing the inner voice's thoughts, move to its chair. When voicing your own, move back to your own chair. This physical separation, using two chairs, will help you more clearly differentiate between your conscious position and your unconscious adversarial position.

TECHNIQUE

1. Complete the Relaxation Exercise, spending no more than five minutes.

2. Remember a time when you spoke before a group of people and your anxiety was particularly bad.

3. Allow your inner critical voice to come to mind.

4. "Hear" it as clearly as you can.

5. Assume "its" chair.

6. Allow yourself to "be" this critical voice.

Let your body, your emotions, your tone of voice, be the ones it uses when talking to you.

7. Using its intention and tone of voice, say aloud what it is now saying to you as you wish to express yourself before others.

8. Hold nothing back.

9. Let it say its worst.

10. Listen to what it has to say, the way in which it says it.

11. If it wants to express something physically, it may do so.

12. Now, allow it to have impact on you, and acknowledge your reactions to what it has to say.

13. Assume your own chair, and answer this voice.

14. Go with your first impulse.

15. Respond from your deepest level of being.

16. Say what you want, behave as you choose.

Do not judge what emerges from either your conscious or your unconscious voice.

Accept whatever comes up. Go as far as you can.

17. Does it want to respond to you?

18. If so, again assuming its chair, do so.

19. Do you want to reply?

20. If so, sitting in your own chair, do so.

21. Keep the dialogue going, assuming the chair of the appropriate speaker each time you speak.

You will know when the energy generated by the exercise is exhausted because there will be a flatness and repetitiveness to the experience. This will indicate that for now this is as far as you can go. Stay with the dialogue only as long as it feels spontaneous. It is better to stop than to fake it.

When the exercise feels flat, say good-bye.

Afterward write down as much of the dialogue as you can and any reactions you may have to the exercise.

Before you leave your workshop, give yourself time to become readjusted to everyday life.

If you have found that you were unable to stand up for yourself against this inner voice (Steve's experience during his first attempt), then try to examine why you cannot do so.

22. For example, do you agree with what it tells you?

23. In what ways?

24. What would make it possible for you to stand up to its negativity?

If you can't answer this last question, perhaps you need to reexamine what you may be getting out of being so afraid. Return to Exercise #8 and work on the questions.

When you have done so, try again to answer the questions in this exercise that stumped you before.

———————————— ▬ ————————————

Answers to these questions will help you develop the strength to confront your inner adversarial voices so that you can deprive them of their silencing energy.

This is a particularly important exercise because it gives you the device with which you can confront your own self-sabotage.

We think of ourselves as a single entity, but in reality the human personality comprises many facets, some of which are known and a great many of which are unknown. We cannot alter something of which we are unaware, but when we bring unknown psychological material into consciousness, we can influence and change its impact.

The inner energy that you have called forth in these exercises, experienced as a voice or a person or animal, represents parts of your personality that terrorize you and force you to remain self-conscious, silent, and anxious when you wish to be heard and seen.

They do so by convincing you that you are stupid, or untalented, or boring, or unlovable, and that your shortcomings will be readily visible for everyone to see. And the shame that is so often a component of performances anxiety is the by-product of believing these "voices"—believing that you are valueless and deserving of punishment.

Sometimes, when you do this last exercise, a familiar inner voice may appear; sometimes the voice will be unfamiliar. All these critical voices need to be energized, fleshed out, and confronted individually and repeatedly. For it is through repeated confrontation with your own terrorizing inner energy that you will diminish your performance anxiety.

There is no end to the power of this exercise. You can return to it whenever your inner voices come up to bedevil you, and you will always find it effective in neutralizing their energy.

Just as you have spent years reinforcing your old ways of being, so you will have to reinforce this new ability to support your true self. You do not have to continue to

re-create patterns established in childhood, but it will require repeated action on your part to change these patterns
and establish new ones.

You have now completed your workshop series.

Allow yourself to acknowledge all that you have accomplished, and celebrate your achievements.

I hope you are very proud of yourself. You deserve to be.
I know the price that this work can exact, and I applaud your
tenacity, honesty, and courage.

REINFORCING YOUR GAINS IN THE
MONTHS TO COME

I have given you an enormous amount of material in this
chapter.

Please remember that it would take six weeks of intensive
work to complete all these exercises in a group workshop. It
will take most people almost twice that time to thoroughly
undertake these exercises at home. If you are unused to
inner exploration, you may find that you prefer to work
even more slowly.

This is not a contest to see who comes in first. If you need
more time, take it. Taking what you need will increase your
feeling of well-being, for you will be responding to your own
needs.

Even if you can only begin to get into the exercises, you
will have accomplished something of which you can be
proud. Begin again where you stopped, and try to do a little
more each time.

Respect your resistance, your fear.

Our terrors have real power over us whether or not the

outer catalysts are now valid. They are to be acknowledged and respected because they were come by honestly. They function as the best we could do to take care of ourselves and survive in what we still perceive to be a dangerous and hostile environment.

We will not give up our defenses without a struggle.

We have to convince ourselves that it is safe for us to come out of hiding, or we will continue to be afraid to do so.

Give yourself some time off and then return to your notes and your answers. Make note of any changes you have observed in your experience of self-exposure or self-support.

If after reflection you feel that a particular exercise has more to give you, go back and repeat it, beginning again with the Relaxation Exercise. You may want to repeat it more than once. Trust yourself and continue to follow your psyche's lead.

When your inner adversarial voices come up, confront them immediately. Then and there dialogue with them in your mind as you have been taught. I still do this myself whenever necessary, and it is amazingly effective. Within a few exchanges the voices lose their power and I experience a release of emotion and a new resolve to get on with it.

For example, there were many times during the long writing of this book when my inner critic would ask me, "What makes you think anyone would want to read what you've written?" Each time the question arose it would stop me and I would be disheartened. But being aware of my own inner critic, and knowing the effectiveness of this technique, I was able after a moment to answer, "That's okay. I want to do it anyway." And when I did so, I could feel a release and a rush of energy; the negative voice dissolved immediately, and I was able to get back to my writing.

Remember, in order to alter our patterns of reaction and behavior we must first become conscious of them. But we cannot settle for insight alone. Understanding without action is of no value here.

For our anxiety to diminish or disappear, we must use what we have discovered from our inner explorations to confront and stand against the parts of our self that sabotage us.

Keep working.

FORMING LEADERLESS GROUPS

Whatever the extent of your shyness and self-consciousness, you will find that both diminish, and your relatedness grows, as you work on your fear of the judgments of others. And you may now learn to your surprise that people you've known for a long time also suffer from performance anxiety and have tried to hide it, just as you have.

Perhaps you may now wish to join with them so that you can work on these exercises together. In such groups the others automatically become "audience," which will give you a chance to further enhance your skills.

Leaderless group work can be very effective. Keep the group small—no more than four people—so that each participant will have a chance to be seen and heard at each session. (Even two people, each working in turn, can constitute a workshop.)

You might find it helpful to have each member of the group read this book so that you all start with the same understanding of the work to be done.

Make a verbal contract with each other to meet for a certain time for about two hours once a week.

Suggest that each member of the group wear comfortable clothing and bring writing material.

Set your chairs in a circle. Have two extra chairs available for use in the exercises.

Apportion the time so that each of you will get a chance to work on the same exercise during a particular session.

Begin the first meeting by standing, one at a time, and telling the others how your performance anxiety manifests and what you hope to get out of the workshop.

Work on the exercises in the same order in which they appear in this book. In addition to being done as individual exercises, they may take the form of questions that might be used for group discussion.

Choose the person to begin, and continue around in order. The following session, begin with the next person, and continue in this way until all of you have had both the experience of being first and the tension of having to wait because you are last.

Be careful that feedback is used only to clarify what has been evoked by the exercise.

Don't analyze or make suggestions about each other's work—just receive the work and support each other's efforts. You know how hard it is to do these exercises, and encouragement helps foster courage.

Sometimes one person will attempt to dominate a group (out of an unconscious need for control because of fear), and that interferes with the climate of safety that others need for concentration on the work. If you have set up a format for equality during the first session, this is less likely to happen, but if it does, the group can confront the issue together.

You are all in the same boat—you all know what your fear costs you. And you know it takes discipline to do this work. No matter how far someone gets in the exercises, or where the exercises lead, support yourself and each other and keep working.

These exercises have proved their effectiveness for many other people. If you keep working on them, I assure you they will produce results for you, too.

SEEKING PROFESSIONAL HELP

This inner work can bring up thoughts and feelings that may be too painful or anxiety provoking for you to carry alone. If this happens, please seek professional psychological help.

Performance anxiety is not something of which to be ashamed. It is a treatable psychological disorder and not a sign of weakness. Ask your doctor or your local hospital for a referral to a trained professional.

There is no shame in being so afraid, but it would be a shame to waste your life hiding in the shadows.

Learn as much as you can about your disorder and the available forms of treatment. (The bibliography may be of help to you.)

And get treatment. You don't have to spend the rest of your life with this affliction.

Expanding Consciousness

———

Every individual needs revolution, inner division, over-throw of the existing order, and renewal. . . . Individual self-reflection, return of the individual to the ground of human nature, to his own deepest being with its individual and social destiny—here is the beginning of a cure.
—C. G. JUNG

OUR ATTACKS OF PERFORMANCE anxiety command our attention, and I believe that this is what they have been designed by the psyche to do. If we don't try to avoid or anesthetize our anxiety, but rather accept these attacks as goal-oriented communication from our inner source, we are led to investigate the unconscious. Through inner reflection we discover parts of our personality that are striving to be lived in consciousness, parts that, when acknowledged, make us more complete and authentic.

Our performance anxiety, then, may be seen to have had the intention of making us more conscious.

Ancient peoples projected unconscious parts of the psyche onto their gods. When they were overwhelmed by a mood or emotion, they declared themselves invaded by the god whose essence they were experiencing.

The Greeks, in the case of an attack of panic, would have said that they had been invaded by the great nature god, Pan, the personification in Greek religion of untamed instinct—that is, instinct before it was altered through adaptation. During an attack of panic, Pan's essence—untamed instinct—has overwhelmed the ego, with its illusion of control. "I want," "I will do," are useless.

As we face our panic rather than flee from it (as did Pan's nymphs), we give up our bodiless outer vigilance and reflective need to please and are able to turn our attention toward inner reflection—toward self-reflection.

With introspection, by asking ourself questions and struggling for truthful answers, we quiet the ego, formerly flitting and flying in fear. From this place of quiet reflection, Pan's essence can emerge, not as the god who overwhelms, but as the god who connects us with our instinctual nature in the body.

Pan's myth helps us to see that in panic our repressed authentic impulses and reactions break out of their adaptive bondage.

If we are to return to a natural ground of being and avoid a life of mere existence—a life where we are always "doing" rather than "being"—we must free ourselves from our patterns of repression.

By confronting and owning the material that has been habitually repressed and projected, we allow back into consciousness more of the angry, fearful, and split-off true feelings that originated in childhood.

We become able to acknowledge our silencing of our self that is the result of our having been silenced. We see that not only have we been abused, we have become self-abusers;

not only criticized, we have become the never-to-be-satisfied self-critic.

This is a bitter bill for most of us who prefer the illusion of our innocence. But if we can accept those parts of ourselves that don't live up to our one-sidedly admirable image of our self, we are no longer trapped in the helplessness and victimization of childhood. Less noble than we imagined ourselves to be, with the inclusion of formerly unconscious material and the withdrawal of projections, consciousness is enlarged and we go forth stronger and more authentic.

The importance of our consciousness cannot be overemphasized.

Our world is threatened because we are threatening. When we can accept that as part of our humanity we are both good and bad, capable of the highest goodwill and the lowest of evil intentions—capable even, under certain circumstances, of acting out of our darkest places—then we no longer see the dark side of ourselves in projection. By acknowledging our own darkness, we see it is not our neighbors (or neighboring country), nor people of other races, genders, religions, or sexual persuasions who are the enemy. The enemy is within each of us.

Our responsibility as human beings is to live our lives as consciously, as authentically, as possible.

It is an urgent task, for we hold the future of the planet in our hands.

It is a task that begins with self-confrontation.

Bibliography

———

Beard, Philip. "Introduction." *Bulletin of the Menninger Clinic* (spring 1994): 58/2 (supp. A).

Bion, Wilfred R. *Second Thoughts*. London: Maresfield Library, 1990.

Bulletin of the Menninger Clinic (spring 1992): 56/2 (supp. A), "Integrated Treatment of Panic Disorder and Social Phobia."

———. (spring 1994): 58/2 (supp. A), "Fear of Humiliation: Integrated Treatment of Social Phobia and Comorbid Considerations."

Fairbairn, W. Ronald D. *Psychoanalytic Studies of the Personality*. London: Tavistock Publications Ltd./Routledge & Kegan, Paul, Ltd., 1952.

Greven, Philip. *Spare the Child: The Religious Roots of Punishment and the Psychologic al Impact of Physical Abuse*. New York: Alfred A. Knopf, 1991.

Grotstein, James S. *Splitting and Projective Identification*. Northvale, N.J.: Jason Aronson, Inc., 1986.

Guntrip, Harry. *Schizoid Phenomena Object-Relations and the Self*. New York: International Universities Press, Inc., 1969.

———. "The Schizoid Problem." In *Psychoanalytic Theory, Therapy, and the Self*. New York: Basic Books, 1971, 1973.

Jung, Carl G. *The Collected Works* (Bollingen Series XX), 20 vols. Princeton, N.J.: Princeton University Press, 1953–1979.

———. *Analytical Psychology, Notes of the Seminar Given in 1925.* Princeton, N.J.: Princeton University Press, 1989.

———. *The Visions Seminars* (1934), vol. 2. New York: Spring Publications, 1976.

———. *Letters,* vol. 1, 1906–1950. Princeton, N.J.: Princeton University Press, 1973.

Kahan, Hazel. *Stage Fright in the United States.* Summary of Bruskin/Goldring Ominpol Research, 1993.

Kohut, Heinz. *The Analysis of the Self.* Madison, Conn.: International Universities Press, Inc., 1971.

Marshall, John R. *Social Phobia: From Shyness to Stage Fright.* New York: Basic Books, 1994.

Miller, Alice. *For Your Own Good.* New York: The Noonday Press, 1990.

Miller, Susan. *The Shame Experience.* Hillsdale, N.J.: The Analytic Press, 1993.

Montejo, Julieta, and Michael R. Liebowitz. "Social Phobia: Anxiety Disorder and Comorbidity." *Bulletin of the Menninger Clinic* (spring 1994): 58/2 (supp. A).

Nathanson, Donald, ed. *The Many Faces of Shame.* New York: The Guilford Press, 1987.

Olivier, Laurence. *Confessions of an Actor.* New York: Simon & Schuster, 1982.

———. *On Acting.* New York: Simon & Schuster, 1986.

Osborne, John. *Almost a Gentleman,* vol. 2, 1955–1966. London: Laber & Fabe, Ltd., 1991.

Perera, Sylvia Brinton. *Descent to the Goddess: A Way of Initiation for Women.* Toronto, Canada: Inner City Books, 1981.

Spoto, Donald. *Laurence Olivier, A Biography.* New York: HarperCollins, 1992.

Stern, Daniel N. *The Interpersonal World of the Infant.* New York: Basic Books, Inc., 1985.

Stolorow, Robert D., and Frank M. Lachmann. *Psychoanalysis of Developmental Arrests: Theory and Treatment.* Madison, Conn.: International Universities Press, Inc., 1980.

Whitmont, Edward C. *The Alchemy of Healing: Psyche and Soma.* Berkeley, Calif.: North Atlantic Books, 1993.

Wickes, Frances G. *The Inner World of Childhood.* Englewood Cliffs, N.J.: Prentice-Hall, Inc., 1966.

Winnicott, D. W. *The Maturational Process and the Facilitating Environment.* New York: International Universities Press, Inc., 1965.

———. *Playing and Reality.* London: Tavistock Publications, Ltd., 1971.

Zerbe, Kathryn J. "Uncharted Waters: Psychodynamic Considerations in the Diagnosis and Treatment of Social Phobia." *Bulletin of the Menninger Clinic* (spring 1994): 58/2 (supp. A).